How to Obtain Financial Freedom Work Book

Unless otherwise indicated, all Scriptures references, are taken from the King James Version of the Bible

ISBN 978-0-9821450-7-4

Copyright © 2011 by CLM Publication & Publishing Ministries

Published by CLM Publication & Publishing Ministries
P.O. Box 932
Chesterfield, VA 23832

Printed in the United States of America; All rights reserved under International Copyright Law. Contents and cover may not be reproduced in whole or in part in any form without the expressed written consent of the publisher.

How to Obtain Financial Freedom Work Book

All rights reserved. No part of this book may be reproduced without written permission from the publisher except for use of brief review for further of the Kingdom of God unless otherwise indicated, all Scriptures are taken from the King James Version of the Bible

CLM Publications, & Publishing, LLC

P.O. Box 932

Chesterfield, VA 23832

www.CLMPublications.info

ISBN 978-0-9821450-7-4

Cover Design/Graphics: Shelly E. Middleton

Author: James L. Monteria

Associate Editor: Lisa Jones

Published by CLM Publications & Publishing, LLC

Copyright © 2011 by CLM Publication & Publishing, LLC Printed in the United States of America; All rights reserved under International Copyright Law. Contents and cover may not be reproduced in whole or in part in any form without the expressed written consent of the publisher.

How to Obtain Financial Freedom

Did you know that God has a "Master Plan" that enables His children to experience financial freedom? Did you know that Your Heavenly Father has made available His "Glory Team" to help you obtain and walk in financial freedom? God wants to open up the whole realm of His nature and put it on display.

He says in Deuteronomy 8:18 (KJV) *"But thou shalt remember the Lord thy God: for it is he that giveth thee power to get wealth, that he may establish his covenant which he sware unto thy fathers, as it is this day."* Also, 3 John 2(KJV) states *"Beloved, I wish above all things that thou mayest prosper and be in health, even as thy soul prospereth."* God desires that His children prosper and He gave us power to get wealth because He has a plan. Yes! The Bible is clear that God has a plan for your money. If you are not handling your finances in line with God's plan, then your whole life is out of order.

No matter how spiritual you may be in other areas, you will never know the real blessing and oversight of God in your life until you bring your money in line with the will of God as revealed in His Word. Just as the caterpillar on the cover of this manual has to go through the process of metamorphosis to become a butterfly, we as citizens of the Kingdom of God have to follow His process of how we are to view and use money. The pages in this manual will enlighten you and also challenge you to follow God's "Master Plan" for your finances in faith and obedience. Are you ready to obtain your financial freedom? The Master and His "Glory Team" are waiting for you!

Table of Contents

Acknowledgment — Page VI

Guidelines for Study — Page VII

Section I

Some <u>Natural Things</u> that you *Need* to Know in Order to become "Financial Literate" that we may "Obtain Financial Freedom"

Introduction — Page 1

Chapter 1 - *We must have a <u>Mindset</u> to be Prosperous* — Page 2

Chapter 2 - <u>Natural Things</u> You Need To Know In Order to "Obtain Financial Freedom" — Page 12

1. Identifying Financial Goals/Making Plans (10-10-80) — Page 13
2. Budgeting — Page 15
3. Banking / Interest Rates / ATM Fees and Credit Unions — Page 16
4. Borrowing To Manage Your Debt, Credit Reports, and Scores — Page 18
5. Credit Cards verse Debit Cards — Page 21
6. BUYING or LEASING a car, shopping for your target price. — Page 24
7. Health Insurance — Page 26
8. Life Insurance — Page 28
9. Auto Insurance — Page 31
10. Renter Insurance — Page 32

Section II

What are the **Levels** you need to know in Order to "Build" A Strong **Financial House.** A strong financial house has each **seven level**. Everything in life must be done in decency and order. On a scale of 1–10, how strong is your financial house?

First Level of a Strong Financial House - Goals and Dreams	Page 35
Second Level of a Strong Financial House - Emergency Account	Page 35
Third Level of a Strong Financial House - Protection Management	Page 36
Fourth Level of a Strong Financial House - Budgeting	Page 37
Fifth Level of a Strong Financial House - Debt Management	Page 38
Sixth Level of a Strong Financial House – Education\Retirement	Page 39
Seventh Level of a Strong Financial House - Review levels 1-6	Page 40

Section III

The **Spiritual things** you need to know in Order To "Build" a Strong **Financial House, and** "How to obtain *Financial*"

Chapter 3 - *There Are Two Kingdoms on Planet Earth!*	Page 42
Chapter 4 - *The Master Plan of God and the Glory Team*	Page 50
Chapter 5 - *Stewardship and the Kingdom of God*	Page 56
Chapter 6 - *Tithing (10%)*	Page 64
Chapter 7 - *Offerings*	Page 69
Chapter 8 - *The Principle of First-fruits*	Page 72
Chapter 9 - *The Principle of Sowing and Reaping*	Page 76
Chapter 10 - *Everybody Has A Seed!*	Page 79
Chapter 11 - *Tracking Your Seed*	Page 83

Section IV

Kingdom of darkness – *The devil diabolical plan is to bring humans into bondage through the influence of his demonic forces operating behind the scenes:*

Chapter 12 – The "Rat Pack from Hell	Page 89
The Spirit of Mammon	Page 87
The Spirit of Greed	Page 93
The Spirit of Poverty	Page 98

Section V

The chose is yours. *God has provided a way for us to break free of the world system, and fulfill our destiny.*

Chapter 13 - *Switching Systems*	Page 103
Chapter 14 – *Investing in the Kingdom of God*	Page 113
Chapter 15 - *The True Reason for Prosperity*	Page 116
Appendix A: *Keys to the Kingdom of Heaven*	Page 120
Appendix B: *Testimony of What a $500 Seed Can Do*	Page 124
Appendix C: *Example of a Small church with 250 members who tithes 250 Members Who Tithe*	Page 126
Appendix D: *A Successful strategy for raising large Gift small Ministries*	Page 127
Appendix E: **How to Open a Checking Account: Step - by - Step Guide**	
	Page 129
Endnotes	Page 135
Decision	Page 136
About the Author	Page 138

Acknowledgement

First, foremost, I would not even know God, or be able to write anything about Him, were it not for His grace and mercy! I have come to appreciate the grace of God, the Lordship of Jesus Christ, and the Holy Spirit's presence in my life and my ministry, even more than words could express.

Secondly, I am blessed to have a supportive and loving wife, Sonja, who encourages me to be and do all that God has put in my heart. I am thankful to have two wonderful parents, Jimmie and Ora Monteria, who instilled values, confidence, and an "all things are possible" attitude in me as a child.

Thirdly, I am deeply indebted to many people the Lord has used to teach and enlighten me on simple basic truths from the Word of God. I want to thank Dr. Frederick K.C. Price and the staff of Every Increasing Faith ministries who are the primary people the Lord used to lead me into a personal relationship with Jesus Christ. I want to thank Mrs. Hughes and Mrs. Carter who the Lord used to help me build my personal relationship with Jesus Christ. Their example of love for Jesus, and their 'feeding me' through Bible study and prayer meetings was instrumental in my becoming established in Christ! I am eternally grateful for the both of them.

Also, I would like to acknowledge *Pastor Clinton and Sarah Utterback and the Redeeming Love Christian Center staff*. As a new Christian, they helped to establish my heart in the basics of the Bible. They taught me how to spend time in the Word of God, how to esteem God's Word, how to grow in Christ, how to walk by faith, and how to be a witness for Him. I appreciate all that they put into my early Christian life.

Finally, I want to thank the following people, who through the years, have played an instrumental role in helping me grow, in leading me into the Spirit-filled life, and in teaching me the redemptive realities that believer's have in Christ.

> Mrs. Essmae Callis, Mrs. Maybel Callis, Pastor Bob Yandian and Grace Fellowship, Dr. Fredrick K C Price, Dr. Leroy Thompson, Pastor Bill Winston and Ms. Cynthia, Ms. Shelly Middleton and Ms. Lisa Jones of Rejoyce in Jesus Ministries, Kenneth E Hagin and the Faculty of Rhema Bible Training Center

GUIDELINES FOR STUDY

A. Guidelines for Individual Study

1. Set aside a regular time each week when you can get alone with God and study the lessons in this workbook.
2. Pray and ask the Lord to illuminate His Word to you as you study.
3. Look up each scripture and take time to think about (meditate on) the Word of God.
4. Move through the book at a steady pace and allow the Holy Spirit to minister to you personally.

B. Guidelines for Group Study

1. In group study, it is important to have one leader, preferably a mature Christian, who can facilitate the study each week.
2. Determine a regular time and a quiet location for weekly group meetings to study the lessons in this workbook.
3. Pray and ask the Lord to illuminate His Word each week.
4. Look up the scriptures and take turns reading them aloud.
5. Encourage each person to participate. Do not allow one person to dominate the discussion.
6. Allow for group discussion and interaction during the lessons, but avoid distractions with unnecessary side issues.
7. Don't be in a hurry to complete the workbook; rather, maintain a steady pace through the lesson while allowing the Holy Spirit the freedom to minister to each individual in the group.
8. Assign the next lesson as homework each week. After the group members have completed their individual study, they will be more familiar with the material. Encourage group members to write down any questions they have and present them for discussion the next time you meet together.

Deuteronomy 8:18 (KJV)

"¹⁸But thou shalt remember the LORD thy God: for it is he that giveth thee power to get wealth that he may establish his covenant which he sware unto thy fathers, as it is this day."

John 10:10 (KJV)

"I am come that they might have life, and that they might have it more abundantly"

2 Corinthians 8:9 (KJV)

"⁹For ye know the grace of our Lord Jesus Christ, that, though he was rich, yet for your sakes he became poor, that ye through his poverty might be rich.

3 John 1:2 (KJV)

"²Beloved, I wish above all things that thou mayest prosper and be in health, even as thy soul prospereth.

Part I
Building a Strong Financial House

Natural Things you need to know in Order To "build"

A Strong <u>Financial</u> House

Introduction

Most books dealing with how to obtain financial freedom usually share how you are to live within your means, like in the example of Income versus Expenses and a Budget Plan for a small business. In this book, I want to go behind the screen and reveal what is happening from a spiritual perspective. By understanding what is happening from a spiritual perspective, we will better understand what is happening in the natural world.

Money is rarely the root cause of stress in many lives; rather, it is the attitude toward money that causes the problem. When it comes to materialism or material things, Paul wrote that he had learned to be content, according *Philippians 4:11-13*: "*¹¹Not that I speak in respect of want: for I have learned, in whatsoever state I am, therewith to be content. ¹²I know both how to be abased, and I know how to abound: everywhere and in all things I am instructed both to be full and to be hungry, both to abound and to <u>suffer</u> need. ¹³I can do all things through Christ which strengtheneth me.*"

> *...Study to shew thyself approved unto God, a workman that needeth not to be ashamed, rightly dividing the word of truth.*
> *2 Timothy 2:15(KJV)*

> *...All scripture is given by inspiration of God, and is profitable for doctrine, for reproof, for correction, for instruction in righteousness*
> *2 Timothy 3:16(KJV)*

> *...In meekness instructing those that oppose themselves; if God peradventure will give them repentance to the acknowledging of the truth; 26And that they may recover themselves out of the snare of the devil, who are taken captive by him at his will.*
> *2 Timothy 2:25, 26 (KJV)*

Chapter 1
We must have a <u>Mindset</u> to be Prosperous

When thinking about *How To Obtain Financial Freedom,* a scripture comes to mind that, to me, represents financial freedom and the abundant life God has for His children:

> "²Beloved, I wish above all things that thou mayest prosper and be in **health**, even as thy soul prospereth" *(3 John 1:2).*

Most people want a lot of money, but do not realize the danger of having it. Consider the story about how money came by a couple's house one day. The couple, at home one day, heard a knock at the front door. Hearing the knock, the husband went to answer the door. To his surprise, Money was standing there. The husband invited Money in, and Money took a seat on their sofa. As husband, wife and Money sat together; Money began to share his heart. *I am blamed for everything,* he complained. *I am only money, a tool to help you to do what you want,* he said, *and I get blamed for everything.*

Money is neither good nor bad. Rather, it is only what a person does with money that makes it meaningful or not.

As an earthly father, my children have asked for money to purchase things that they were not ready to handle. As any good father, I chose not to give them the money, not because I lacked the money to give, but because I loved them, and knew the money would be used to do something that was not in their best interests. Our loving Heavenly Father is much wiser than our earthly parents are.

It is only as our soul prospers and matures that we will be blessed with abundance. I want you to know beyond any shadow of doubt – it *is the will of our heavenly Father to bless us with abundance.*

In order for us to understand the *full* meaning of *3 John 1:2,* we must first understand some of the basic principles of how man was created.

Human Beings are Spirit, Soul, and Body

Examining the Word of God helps us to understand the makeup of mankind: man is a spirit, has a soul, and lives in a physical body.

In Accordance to *1Thessalonians 5:23*, says...

> "*23And the very God of peace sanctify you wholly; and I pray God your whole spirit and soul and body be preserved blameless unto the coming of our Lord Jesus Christ*"

We understand that we were created in the very image and likeness of God (*Genesis 1:26*) and, because God is a Spirit (*John 4:24*), we can conclude that we also are spirits. When a person is born-again, our Spirit is recreated. Our natural bodies remain the same until the return of Christ. The Soul has not been saved, but must be restored.

We have a Soul - Along with *1 Thessalonians 5:23*, we have *Hebrews 4:12* - "For the word of God is quick, and powerful, and sharper than any two-edged sword, piercing even to the dividing asunder of soul and spirit, and of the joints and marrow, and is a discerner of the thoughts and intents of the heart." This tells us clearly that while the soul and spirit may be joined together, they are not the same thing and can be divided or separated.

Defining the Soul - Now that we understand that man is a spirit, has a soul and lives in a body, it is important to us that we understand exactly what the soul is. The original text (written in ancient Greek) uses the word "*psuche*" that is translated into Modern English as "*soul.*"

Vine's Dictionary of Greek defines the soul as "the seat of Intellect": the seat of the sentient element in man, which he perceives, reflects, feels, and desires. The soul is the place that houses our will, our emotions, and our intellect (the thinking, reasoning part of us: The Mind).

Our souls was damage by the fall of Adam and Eve. Our souls have also been wounded by the hurt that we have experienced in life. Many life experiences can leave behind broken and wounded hearts. Whether hurtful words, abandonment, or separation from a loved one, these experiences wound our souls. Making decisions out of a wounded soul will only lead us to make wrong decisions.

Psalm 23:3 teaches that "[God] restoreth the soul," and *James 1:21* teaches that "Wherefore lay apart all filthiness and superfluity of naughtiness, and receive with meekness the engrafted word, which is able to save your souls. See it is through mediating and studying the Word of God that our souls are saved. In *1 Peter 1:9;* we learn about the "salvation of our souls." God bless us with a new spirit the moment you except Jesus Christ as you Lord and Saviour. We as believers are responsible for the salvation of our soul, in other, we must be doer of the Word of God in order to save or restore our souls.

This is done through reading, observing (*Joshua 1:8*); studying (*2 Timothy 2:15*); and mediating (*Psalm 1:1-3*); on what we read, hear, and see pertaining to God. As you mature in the soul, then and only then will God (?) entrust us with more. I need to make this point This is done through reading, observing (*Joshua 1:8*); studying (*2 Timothy 2:15*); and mediating (*Psalm 1:1-3*); on what we read, hear, and see pertaining to God. As you mature in the soul, then and only then will God (?) entrust us with more. I need to make this point clear: when I talk about "even as your soul prospers" I am not only talking about financial prosperity, but also in every area of life.

I defined five different aspects of prosperous life:

(1) **Spiritual Prosperity** - being born-again (John 3:16),

(2) **Soul Prosperity** - being made whole and at peace in your mind and emotions (Romans 12:2);

(3) **Physical Prosperity** - being made whole in your physical body and walking in divine health (Isaiah 53:5-6);

(4) **Social Prosperity** - one who has status in the community, the go to person.

(5) **Financial Prosperity** – being in a position to not only meet your need, but also those of others (Malachi 3:8-12; 3 John 2).

As we have said before: man is spirit, has a soul, and lives in a body. There are so many theories about the soul of man. Every religion has its personal opinion about the soul. What do we as Christians believe about the soul? Failing to understand this significant difference can lead only to confusion and as in the case of most Christians to **ERROR**.

The soul of a man is made up of three compartments:
  (1) The Mind,
  (2) The Will,
  (3) The Emotions,

All four of these compartments make their home in the human brain. These all relate to how our brain works. Our focus is on the mind, please see list of the functionality of each area within the soul.

The Mind - The mind is that part of us that decides what and how we think. Our thoughts are developed by various stimuli such as environment, education, giftedness, what you see, what you hear, and what you read, etc. The mind houses what we know about everything. Our mind is filled with memories, information, and data. Everything that you have ever seen has been down loaded onto your hard drive file of your mind. The mind allows us to reason and determines our reasoning skills and patterns. Therefore, if someone is determined to be out of their mind, we usually mean that they are not able to reason properly.

The Will - Our will consists of what we will allow or accept. Our will also is connected to what we determine to do, to endure, or the degree of pursuit in which we go after something. The will is attached to our desires concerning, people, places or things.

We do those things that we are willing to do. It is called "free will." When the minister asks the bride, will you take this man to be your husband, she says, "I will."

The Emotions - Our emotions tell us how we feel about events, experiences, or various stimuli. The emotions we feel are then manifested through words, expressions, and actions. Our emotions can be deceiving and sometimes an enemy to our faith. Emotions are a gift from God. We must understand the concept that our emotions must be spiritually controlled. See prior to become a Christians most of our decision were made base on our feeling.

The Christian must understand that our spirit, soul, and body have been connected in a way that it is hard to separate one from the other. Only the Word of God can separate Spirit and Soul according to *Hebrews 4:12*.

HOW DO WE HAVE A PROSPEROUS SOUL?

We must stop being programmed by the world's systems and allow our minds to become supernaturally transformed. We must be open to the have a kingdom of God mentality, because that is the way of the Kingdom (Kingdom of God lifestyle). A life that is focused and directed by God-kind of thoughts. We need to learn how to think the way that God would have us to think. *Romans 12:2* teaches: "Do not conform any longer to the pattern of this world, but be transformed by the renewing of your mind.

Then you will be able to test and approve what God's will is His good, pleasing and perfect will." Notice again that according to scripture, situations and circumstances can be transformed. When you are considering or thinking about some changes in your life and you apply what the Word of God says to do. This the beginning of the renewing our minds process ("the thinking, reasoning part of us") to what God has promised in His Word, then things will change.

What we think matters:

In According to *Proverbs 23:7*,

"For as a man thinketh in his heart, so is he."

God has stated emphatically that what we think will have a direct effect on us, because the process of making a decision beginning with the thought process and leads to action, whether good or bad. Jesus told us the same thing in Luke 6:45, therefore it is vital that we renew the way we think, and make sure what we think about situation is in agreement with what God has said in His Word about it.

It is important to understand that what we think is based entirely upon what we believe. If our belief is wrong, then our thinking will be wrong. In addition, if our thinking is wrong, then instead of blessings manifesting in our life, we will have something other than the blessing that we desire.

Jesus told us in *Luke 6:45*: "The good man brings good things out of the good stored up in his heart, and the evil (doubtful, unbelieving) man brings evil things out of the evil (doubt and unbelief) stored up in his heart. For out of the overflow of his heart his mouth speaks."

In other words, what we believe in our heart, and what we think in our mind is what we will speak out and talk about. Moreover, when we do: We will experience not what we *want*, not what God has *promised*, but instead we will experience what we have been saying about it.

Therefore if we want to experience the blessing of God in our life, it is vital to us as Christians to speak health and healing, provision and prosperity, deliverance and freedom from affliction, addiction, oppression and depression and anything else that might come our way.

A Prosperous Soul Causes Everything Else to Prosper More often than not, people focus on the wrong things. When trials and troubles come against them all they can think about is the trial and the trouble.

This is why they speak of them so often. When a Christian that has begun to renew his/her mind with the Word of God, their soul begins to prosper and they will speak the Word of God, and the power of God's Word will change (transform) the trouble into blessing as they released faith through Gods Word.

A renew mind which is a part of a Prosper Soul, when facing a trial or trouble they speak the answer rather the problem and the power of God's Word is released and things begin to change!

How Do We Assure That Our Soul Prospers?

     Begin by study and learn the Word of God. Do not just read it: Study it! Ask the Lord for the wisdom to understand it. Ask Him to reveal the truth of the Gospel to you. He Will! When this happens, you will begin to see things as you never saw them before.

You will begin to see all that Christ has purchased for you and what you have in Him as a child of God and an heir of Christ. The result will be that your soul will begin to prosper as scripture has promised, and little by little, you will begin to see changes in your finances, your body, your business, your marriage and your children.

The Bible states clearly, how God thinks about poverty and riches. Poverty is considered a curse, a condition to be pitied and avoided. Repeatedly He warns against neglecting or exploiting the poor.

Poverty is a wretched condition, not a blessing. However, riches are always treated as a dangerous good, a blessing that can easily turn bitter. God knows we have need of money. Poverty is a curse.

In According to *Galatians 3:13-14 says*...

> "*Christ hath redeemed us from the curse of the law, being made a curse for us: for it is written, Cursed is every one that hangeth on a tree: That the blessing of Abraham might come on the Gentiles through Jesus Christ; that we might receive the promise of the Spirit through faith.*"

In the first part of *Deuteronomy 28*, God talks to Israel about the blessings of the Law that will overtake them if they obey His *commands)* vv. 1-14). Then skipping down to verse 15, God says, "But it shall come to pass, if thou wilt NOT hearken unto the voice of the Lord thy God, to observe to do all his commandments and his statutes which I command thee this day; that ALL THESE CURSES shall come upon thee, and overtake thee." The curse or punishment for breaking God's commandments is threefold: poverty, sickness, and the second death.

Deuteronomy 28:16-19, 38-40 "Cursed shalt thou be in the city, and cursed shalt thou be in the field. Cursed shall be thy basket and thy store. Cursed shall be the fruit of thy body, and the fruit of thy land, the increase of thy kine, and the flocks of thy sheep. Cursed shalt thou be when thou comest in, and cursed shalt thou be when thou goest out. Thou shalt carry much seed out into the field, and shalt gather but little in; for the locust shall consume it.

Thou shalt plant vineyards, and dress them, but shalt neither drink of the wine, nor gather the grapes; for the worms shall eat them. Thou shalt have olive trees throughout all thy coasts, but thou shalt not anoint thyself with the oil; for thine olive shall cast his fruit."

Poverty is a curse and not a blessing

You can readily see these verses are talking about poverty and lack. God said poverty and lack was a curse, which was to come upon the people of God because they failed to keep His commandments and His statutes (*Deuteronomy 28:15*).

The curse of poverty should come upon all of us - Gentiles and Jews alike - because all of us have sinned and come short of the glory of God (*Romans 3:23*). However, *Galatians 3:13* tells us that instead of the curse coming upon us, Jesus was made to be a curse for us.

Jesus did not go to the Cross for Himself - He did it for us! The curse fell on Him instead of upon us. He bore the curse for us so we would not have to.

Jesus became our substitute and paid the debt for our sins through His death on the Cross. Moreover, God wrote it down as though we had paid the debt for sin ourselves! Now because of Jesus, we are free from the curse of the Law and that includes the curse of poverty!

> ***In accordance 2 Corinthians, 8:9 says...***
>
> > *"For ye know the grace of our Lord Jesus Christ, that, though he was rich, yet for your sakes he became poor, that ye through his poverty might be rich."*

Some endeavor to put a spiritual interpretation on this verse. They say it is talking about Jesus becoming spiritually poor so we might be made spiritually rich, but there is more to this verse than that.

Although Jesus' needs were always supplied, if He became poor at all, it would only have been from the material standpoint because He never gathered to Himself earthly riches and treasures.

Jesus certainly was not spiritually poor. Someone who was spiritually poor could not work miracles, raise the dead, turn the water into wine, feed five thousand with a little boy's lunch, or heal the sick!

As we come back to the John, Our wish is for all to be prosperous, like the Apostle John's wish for his friend Gaius, is that they might prosper and be in health. However, even more that they "are walking in the truth."

If our souls are prospering, if we are walking in truth, money will play a very small part in our lives, because our focus want be on money simple our needs will be meet, and that is one of the benefits of a prosperous soul.

2 Corinthians 9:8 teaches that "God is able to make all grace abound to you, so that in all things at all times, having all that you need, you will abound in every good work." That is about as comprehensive a promise as anyone could wish for.

1 Timothy 6:6-10 teaches: "But godliness with contentment is great gain. For we brought nothing into the world, and we can take nothing out of it. However, if we have food and clothing, we will be content with that. People who want to get rich fall into temptation and a trap and into many foolish and harmful desires that plunge men into ruin and destruction.

For the love of money is a root of all kinds of evil. Some people, eager for money, have wandered from the faith and pierced themselves with many griefs." *Proverbs 28:6* "Better a poor man whose walk is blameless than a rich man whose ways are perverse." The main thing is always the prosperous soul.

It's true that "The blessing of the LORD brings wealth, and he adds no trouble to it." (*Proverbs 10:22*). God makes his children wealth because their wealth is no threat to their soul, and they understand what the scripture found in Deuteronomy 8:18 means.

For the most part great wealth is a snare and a danger to the soul. As Jesus said, "With what difficulty will the rich man have entering the Kingdom of Heaven!" More often than not, where spiritual things are concerned, God "…has filled the hungry with good things but has sent the rich away empty" (*Luke 1:53*).

However, God intends for us to pay our bills. We are not to be in debt: "Let no debt remain outstanding, except the continuing debt to love one another…" (*Romans 13:8*)

There are many reasons a person might be poor, some are poor because of injustice, through no fault of their own (*Proverbs 10:23*). Some through unwise decisions have fallen into poverty (*Proverbs 11:29; 15:27*); some a result of slothfulness and unwillingness to work (Proverbs *20:13; 18:9*); some may be poor because they have not shown pity on others in need (*Proverbs 21:13*). Some are poor because of their own vices—drugs, alcohol, dishonesty (*Proverbs 20:1; 23:21*).

I do not believe anyone can stay in poverty by which I mean lacking necessities and being unable to pay bills unless there is some condition of the soul that is not prospering. For the promise of God is that He will "supply all of our needs according to the riches of His glory" (*Philippians 4:19*).

Someone may be under a curse of poverty through wrong thinking. Whatever the reason a Christian finds himself either temporarily or permanently in poverty, it is good to look for a spiritual cause; and it most of the times it is a lack of a prosperous soul. **"IT IS GOD'S WILL THAT WE PROSPER"**.

CHAPTER 1 QUESTIONS, "We must have a Mind set to prosper."

True or False

1. True ___ or False ___. Is it the will of God that believers be prosperous?
2. True ___ or False ___. The makeup of man is Spirit, Soul, and Body.
3. True ___ or False ___. When a person is born-again, they get a new Spirit
4. True ___ or False ___. Poverty and lack are curses and not blessings.
5. True ___ or False ___. According to *3 John 1:2*; it is God's will that believers prosper and be in health, even as thy soul prosper.

Fill in the blank

6. There are five different types of prosperity:

    a. _____, b. _____, c. _____,
    d. _____ and e. _____.

7. What are the three compartments of the soul of mankind?

    a. _____, b. _____, and c. _____.

8. As a man thinketh in his _____, so is he.

9. How do we assure that our Soul is prospers? _____.

Multiple Choice

10. What is Soul of mankind is make up what three components?

    A) Mind,
    B) Will,
    C) Emotion,
    D) All of the above.

    ANSWER) _____

Chapter 2
Natural Things You Need to Know in Order to "Obtain Financial Freedom"
Problem/Opportunity

It seem as if money makes the world go around, because vast sums change hands every day in a global economy that affects virtually every man, woman every man, woman and child on the planet. "On a daily basis the Federal Reserve processes around 628,000 FUNDS/Fed Wire transfer transactions. These 628,000 transactions equate to 4 trillion dollars being transfer daily.

Paradoxically, in a time of wealth and opportunity millions of people struggle to survive economically. With consumer credit reaching gigantic proportions, many find themselves mired in debt. Worrying about money matters takes an enormous toll on mental and physical health and general well-being. According to the Census Bureau Poverty, statistics shows that from 1987 – 2005 poverty increased by 12.6 percent.

The Bible Says

- "Training up a child in the way they should go." *Proverbs 22:6*

- "My people are destroyed for lack of knowledge: because thou hast rejected knowledge." *Hosea 4:6a*

- "Therefore my people are gone into captivity, because they have no knowledge." *Isaiah 5:13a*

Natural Things You Need to Know in Order to "Obtain Financial Freedom"

1. <u>**Identifying Financial Goals/Making Plans (10-10-10-70)**</u>

A. **What is the most important first step to take towards achieving your financial goals?** Having a Financial goal are usually categorized as short-term, intermediate, or long-term. A long-term goal of home ownership could entail both short-term and intermediate-term goals; for example, how much to save each month toward a down payment for a home to be bought in five or more years. Must people never set one, therefore, they continue to live from pay check to check!

B. **Financial planners generally show the importance of starting to save and invest early.** What is the main reason for this? The reason for this is because most people wait to late, all of a sudden realize that they do not have enough money live the lifestyle they have become accustom to. The result they in up working longer and for longer.

C. **Save money in a tax-deferred Individual Retirement Account, that earns 8% annually.** A SIMPLE IRA, or Savings Incentive Match Plan for Employees, is a type of traditional IRA for small businesses and self-employed individuals. As with most traditional IRAs, your contributions are tax deductible, and your investments grow tax deferred until you are ready to make withdrawals in retirement.

D. **Whenever you purchase a large expense item plan for it**. Develop a plan that will allow you to be a good steward of what you have, and not over extend yourself? Remember that life is meant to be enjoyed and not being stress out or worrying how you are going to make the necessary payment.

I remember when I got my first car, my dad said, son if you if you get the down payment for the car that you want, I will help you get the car that you want. After working and save up the down payment. My dad and I went to the car dealership and he cosigned for me to get the car. Many years later when I think about how I work and saved every penny to get the down payment, why not work a little longer, about another six months, when I could have pay cash for my car. Once I learned better, I have had the privilege of experiencing paying my vehicles off and not have any payments for five and ten year's periods. Please know there is no shame if you are making payments, but Gods best is to have no payments.

E. **In order to reach a financial goal**. You must set priorities, and am working towards them. Is it a bad thing to change my mind? No, situation in life are constantly changing, so must be flexible.

Natural Things You Need to Know in Order to "Obtain Financial Freedom"

2. **Budgeting** (See page 37)

   A. **The first step in getting your spending under control.** "Consider making a list of the things that you really need as opposed to the things you really want." In this way, you can see where your money is being spent.

   B. **Banking online using personal financial software makes it easier to track your expenses.** By doing this you actual see where you are spending your money. Once you identify the areas that you might be wasting money, make the necessary adjustments and this will help you to live within your budget.

   C. **How much of your income should you aim to save and invest?** As a Christians, I believe that we are to pay tithes (10%) to the local church you are a member of, sow (10%) into good ground, pay yourself (10%) saving, and learn to live off the 70% of your income. If you were working for a company that some type of thrift plan, and the company is willing to match 3%, I would encourage save at least 7%, because with your company willing to match with 3% you will be saving 10% of your income.

   D. **When examining your bank records and you cannot explain why you have withdrawn so much cash, what you should do?** Immediately stop, and make a list of every time you with draw money, because you can become addicted to the ATM machine. (Addicted to Machine)

   E. **The most common cause of spending beyond your means is what? Impulsive buying.** The Rat pack from hell, the spirit of mammon, the spirit of greed, and the spirit poverty. It is a means of worship to these spirits, their influence cause one to spend money contrary to the ways of God meaning that they are not being good stewards over what God has entrust into their care.

Natural Things You Need to Know in Order to "Obtain Financial Freedom"

3. **Banking / Interest Rates / ATM Fees and Credit Unions**

<u>Please</u> know that banks are not your friend, although they provide very friendly customer services. Banks are in business to make money by known, and unknown fees. Choose your bank carefully. *(See Appendix Page 129 How to Open a Checking Account: Step - by - Step Guide)*

> A. **Why is a bank the safest place to keep your money?** Bank deposits are insured by the federal government, and Bank deposits are insured by the federal government. If a U.S. bank goes bust, depositors get their money back up to $ 350,000 per type of account.
>
> B. **The best way to get the most competitive interest rate on a bank CD or credit card is to?** Call the banks in your area. The Internet is the best and easiest way to go when you want to compare rates or deal from banks.
>
> C. **Money taking before CD maturity will cost you what?** "Pay the IRS a penalty, typically 10 percent of the account's value." "Pay the bank a penalty, typically three months' interest."
>
> D. **How often do most banks review and possibly change the interest rates they pay on savings and checking accounts?** "Weekly." Banks often review the interest rates they pay each week. They do not necessarily change rates that often, but they can. That means the rate that is offered when you open your account may be dramatically different a year later, or even a month later.
>
> E. **If you want to get a guaranteed interest rate on a bank deposit for up to five years what must do?** "Take out a mortgage from the same bank." "Put your money in a certificate of deposit." If you buy a fixed-rate, five-year CD you will lock in an interest rate for five years. If during that period, interest rates fall, the bank is stuck with paying you the higher rate it promised. If interest rates rise, you are stuck with the lower rate you agreed to.

F. **When shopping for the best interest-bearing account, the only way to make a true apple-to apples comparison is to review each account's "Annual percentage yield."** Banks frequently use different methods to calculate interest, but APYs are calculated the same way everywhere. As for other numbers, they can vary from bank to bank. Minimum balances can be in force at all times or can be based on averages calculated over a month. Account fees vary depending on how much money you have on deposit and how often you will use the bank's services.

G. **The longer you lock up your money in a CD, the higher the interest rate you will get.** The shorter the term of the CD, the lower the rate. But if you think you might need the cash, buying a short term CD will help you avoid penalties for early withdrawal, and you'll still do better than if you let the money sit in a low-yield savings account.

H. **There are a lot of ways to get a free checking account, but only way that will not work?** If you open a credit union checking account, what might you expect? "Have your paycheck deposited directly into your account." "Limit your use of the bank's services to its tellers." Teller service for checking account customers adds a lot to the bank's expenses. Indeed, some banks offer free checking if you promise not to use the tellers, and if you do, they sock you with a fee if the same transaction could have been conducted at an ATM.

I. **Money market mutual funds are less secure than savings accounts because:** "They are not insured by the federal government." The danger mostly has been theoretical: brokerages and mutual fund companies have usually kick in extra dollars whenever necessary to make sure that customers don't incur losses.

Natural Things You Need to Know in Order "Obtain Financial Freedom"

4. Borrowing To Manage Your Debt, Credit Reports, and Scores.

A. What are the warning signs you have too much debt? There are two other red flags of debt overload:

1. You max out your credit card after paying off the balance;

2. You can only afford to pay the minimum on your credit cards.

Ideally, all your monthly debt, including your mortgage, should amount to no more than how much of your gross income 70%.

- **(10%)** As a Christians you are to pay your tithes
- **(10%)** Seed
- **(10%)** Pay yourself saving
- **(70%)** live off

B. What is the worst kind of debt you can have? Credit cards generally charge the highest interest rates and the interest is not tax deductible.

If you make minimum payments on your credit card balance every month how long, will it take you to pay off this credit card?

C. What should you look for on your credit reports? Your credit reports - and your credit score, which is derive from those reports - are what lenders look at to assess your creditworthiness. All of the factors listed could adversely affect your credit rating. Your credit score is the result of several things: your payment history; how much you owe overall; the length of your credit history; how many new lines of credit you have opened; and the types of credit you have.

D. **When buying a home, should put every dime you have got toward the down payment?** You should never bankrupt yourself for a down payment. You should put down only as much as you can without compromising your emergency cash reserves, and you should have enough to pay closing costs and moving expenses. Be sure to have some left over to cover the cost of maintaining your house once you move in. Even if you have extra cash available on top of a 20 percent down payment, consider whether that money might be put to better use paying off credit card debt. Mortgages, remember, have lower interest rates than credit cards, and mortgage interest is tax deductible.

E. **What is Good debt?** "Borrowing money for anything you really need but cannot afford." Since most of us cannot afford to pay cash for life's big-ticket items, your house and education are good reasons to borrow money. An auto loan or lease might be considered good debt as well; if it is for a car, you need and is not to finance a luxury vehicle that would strain your bank account.

F. **When should you borrow against a 401(k)?** "When you have no other options." Borrowing money from your 401(k) should be your last resort; it may even be better to hit up your relatives before tapping the nest egg. When you borrow from your 401(k), you miss out on two of the biggest advantages to workplace retirement plans: tax-deferred compounding of your money and tax-deductible contributions. Sure, you pay yourself back with interest, but you do so with after-tax dollars. If you quit or lose your job, you will probably have to repay the entire borrowed amount within a few months, if not immediately. If you fail to, you will owe income taxes on the money, plus a 10 percent penalty if you are under 59-1/2.

G. When is it best to take out a home equity loan? "You want to renovate your kitchen." Taking a home equity loan makes the most sense when you are making home improvements that increase the value of your house, such as adding a family room or renovating the kitchen. The interest you pay is deductible and you increase the equity in your home. If you want to pay off your credit card debt, a home-equity loan may work since you are likely to get a lower interest rate and you may deduct the interest on a loan amount up to $ 100,000. Make sure you can afford the monthly payments if you default, you risk losing your home.

Natural Things You Need to Know in Order to "Obtain Financial Freedom"

5. Credit Cards verse Debit Cards

Debit cards: Two ways to use yours

When you shop with your debit card, you are often asked, **"debit or credit?"**

Here are the differences:

Debit: You need to use your PIN (personal identification number) to complete the transaction. The debit option can be used at ATMs and with merchants who accept debit cards.

Use this option when you withdraw cash from an ATM

Credit: You will need to sign a receipt as you do with a credit card. Unlike a credit card purchase, the money is withdrawn directly from your account it is not a loan. The credit option can usually be used if your debit card has a Visa® or MasterCard® logo.

Use this option:

- Most purchases since it may give you extra fraud protection and rewards.
- Purchases at merchants that do not allow an additional cash back withdrawal.

It all comes from the same place. Whether you use the debit or credit option, all purchases made with your debit card are withdrawn directly from your account.

Note: You can use it as a "credit card"

> Do not assume that it helps you build credit, right. Unfortunately, bank accounts only show up on credit reports if you have negative activity, such as overdrawing your account and not paying back your financial institution. Otherwise, you will never see your checking account on your credit report in a positive state

What is great about having a Debit Card?

Convenience: You do not need to carry cash or write checks. In addition, more cash-only retailers now also accept debit cards.

Help avoid interest charges: When you pay with available funds in your account, you will avoid the interest that can come with buying on credit. If you are trying to get out of debt—or avoid getting into it—a debit card can be a good way to go.

What is not so great about having a Debit Card?

A. **Overdraft fees:** You have to be careful not to spend more than is in your account.

B. **Security:** Keep in mind that there may be differences in fraud protection features of debit cards and credit cards, particularly because debit card purchases are withdrawn directly from your checking or savings account.

C. **Caution:** You will need to safeguard your debit card as carefully as your cash. If your card is lost or stolen, report it to your bank immediately to help prevent unauthorized access to your checking or savings account.

Credit cards and debt cards are not the same!

What is great about having a Credit Card?

A. A credit card only offers the credit option a loan you will pay back in the future.

B. **Financial flexibility:** You can make a large purchase, consolidate debt or get emergency funds and pay for them over time, in payments that fit your budget.

C. **Rewards:** You can often earn rewards on purchases when you use a credit card that offers a rewards program.

D. **Security:** This is safest way to shop online since credit cards have stricter limits to fraud liability. Some credit cards also offer purchase protection or extended warranty protection on most of what you buy, online or off.

What is not so great about having a Credit Card?

A. **Too much debt:** Be conscious of what you are spending. The fact that you will have to pay it back so you do not get into more debt than you are comfortable. Interest and fees: Keep in mind that, if you do not pay your bill in full every month, you will be charged interest.

Natural Things You Need to Know in Order to "Obtain Financial Freedom"

6. <u>BUYING or LEASING a car, shopping for your (Money) target price</u>.

Buying and leasing are not the same, when buying a car, you are out-right purchasing it. When leasing a car, it is for a period of time, and then you have an option to buy it or return it back to the leasing company.

Leasing a car rather than buying it will generally cost you much more than simply financing a purchase from the start. If you think, you might want to buy the car, do that from the outset. Lease only if you are sure you do not want to keep the car long term.

If you buy a car or truck, you can postpone any decision about replacing it at least until mechanical trouble forces your hand. If you do not mind driving an older car, the best decision on purely economic grounds usually is to buy a new car and keep on driving it long after your loan payments have stopped.

If you typically trade for a new car every four years or less, you will want to avoid the loan down payment of 10% to 20%, drive close to but not more than the 15,000 miles a year allowed in most leases and typically keep your vehicle in good condition to avoid end-of-lease penalties, you might well be happy leasing.

Keep in mind that there is a reason why those low lease payments look so attractive: Instead of paying for the entire car, you are only paying the estimated depreciation over the time you are leasing it. Therefore, to get a good lease deal, you need to look further than just the payments. You need to understand how leasing works, do your homework, and negotiate as hard as if you were buying the car.

- **A. What percentage of monthly income is reasonable to budget for car expenses**? 10-15% for most people, what percentage of monthly income is reasonable to budget for car expenses.

- **B. What do the comprehensive portion of your auto insurance covers?** "Losses from theft, fire and natural disasters."

- **C. If you buy a three-year-old used car, how much could you save over a new version of the same model?** Cars that hold their value well, like the Toyota Camry, might lose this much in just over a year.

- **D. The capitalized cost of a lease.** "The value of the car at the start of the lease."

E. **When shopping you are likely to get the lowest rate on an auto loan start from?** "Your credit union."

F. **The holdback is a payment.** "The manufacturer to the dealer." Yes. The 2% to 3% holdback is paid periodically to the dealer to help him in financing his inventory.

G. **When should you negotiate, you want to offer to do what?** "A set amount over the dealer's invoice price."

H. **Plan to add state and possibly local sales tax averaging.** The average is "5% to 8%".

I. **What does typical new-car warranty cost, and for how many years?** Three years or 36,000 miles, whichever comes first, is the coverage for most brands.

J. **What does the typical Web buying service gives you what?** The dealer is paying to be the exclusive connection in your area; you typically will get only one dealer contact.

Natural Things You Need to Know in Order to "Obtain Financial Freedom"

7. **Health Insurance**

   A. **What is a Premium?** Your premium is the amount you pay into the insurance plan on a regular basis. If you belong to an employer-sponsored plan, the premium is likely deducted from each paycheck as pre-tax dollars. If you purchase your own health insurance plan, you may have the option to pay your premium annually, quarterly, or monthly. Health insurance premiums vary greatly depending on what medical expenses the plan covers, which doctors you can see, and how much you will have to pay in other ways when you use services.

   Going without health insurance for a while is okay as long as I do not mind risking bankruptcy.

   B. **What is a deductible?** A deductible is the amount I owe out-of-pocket before insurance kick-in and it can range from $100.00 to $2,500 or more.

   C. **What are to be covered by my insurance is Hospital bills?** Preventive care generally is covered by a managed care plan and because keeping you well is one of the ways, managed care cuts cost. With managed care, you can use doctors outside the plan's network depends on the plan.

   D. **What is Catastrophic coverage? It** is Insurance with a high deductible and high maximum payout.

E. **A flexible spending account?** Is a tax-advantaged financial account that can be set up through a cafeteria plan of an employer in the United States. An FSA allows an employee to set aside a portion of earnings to pay for qualified expenses as established in the cafeteria plan, most commonly for medical expenses but often for dependent care or other expenses. Money deducted from an employee's pay into an FSA is not subject to payroll taxes, resulting in substantial payroll tax savings.[1] Before the Patient Protection and Affordable Care Act, one significant disadvantage to using an FSA was that funds not used by the end of the plan year were forfeited to the employer, known as the "use it or lose it" rule. Under the terms of the Affordable Care Act, a plan may permit an employee to carry over up to $500 into the following year without losing the funds.[

F. **What is Co-pay?** Co-pay is the fixed amount you pay for using routine services defined by your plan. For example, some plans charge you a co-pay for visiting your primary care physician, or an emergency room, or purchasing a prescription drug.

G. **What is Out-of-pocket maximum?** Your out-of-pocket maximum is an important feature of your health plan because it limits the total amount you pay each calendar year for healthcare including co-pays, deductibles, and co-insurance. If your policy carries a $2,500 out-of-pocket maximum and you get sick and require many healthcare services, the most you will pay in a year is $2,500. After that, insurance picks up the rest of the tab.

H. **COBRA Insurance?** It gives me the right to keep group coverage but you pay for it yourself.

I. **affordable Health care.gov** A new government health care insurance created by the federal government to all citizens to get affordable health care insurance.

Natural Things You Need to Know in Order to "Obtain Financial Freedom"

8. Life Insurance

For many people, their first experience with life insurance is when a friend or acquaintance gets an insurance license. In my case, a college friend, recently hired by a major insurance company, contacted me (along with all of his other friends) to buy a $10,000 policy underwritten by his company. Unfortunately, however, this is how most people acquire life insurance – they do not buy it, it is sold to them. Life insurance something that you truly need, or is it merely an inconvenience shoved under your nose by a salesperson? While it may seem like the latter is true, there are actually many reasons why you *should* purchase life insurance.

The two basic types of insurance policies. What are they?

Term Life Insurance - Features: Lower premiums with coverage for a specific time frame.

Term life provides coverage for a specific, limited period. Premiums (the amount you pay in) typically increase with age or upon renewal. It is important to understand that if the insured person survives beyond the contract period, no benefit is paid you will not get any money back. For this reason, term life is considered the most cost-effective life insurance.

In the event of a premature death, term life insurance can help:

- Pay off a mortgage
- Replace lost income
- Provide education funds
- Pay funeral and final estate expenses

Permanent Insurance (Whole Life or Ordinary Life). While term insurance is designed to provide protection for a specified time, permanent insurance is designed to provide coverage for your entire lifetime. To keep the premium rate level, the premium at the younger ages exceeds the actual cost of protection. This extra premium builds a reserve (cash value) which helps pay for the policy in later years as the cost of protection rises above the premium.

Whole life policies stretch the cost of insurance over a longer period of time in order to level out the otherwise increasing cost of insurance. Under some policies, premiums are required to be paid for a set number of years. Under other policies, premiums are paid throughout the policyholder's lifetime. The insurance company invests the excess premium dollars

This type of policy, which is sometimes called cash value life insurance, generates a savings element. Cash values are critical to a permanent life insurance policy. The size of the cash value build-up differs from company to company. Sometimes, there is no correlation between the size of the cash value and the premiums paid. It is the cash value of the policy that can be accessed while the policyholder is alive.

Insurance policies cost -There is a huge difference in pricing and products. **Why?** Purchasing a life insurance policy, consider your financial situation and the standard of living you want to maintain for your dependents or survivors. You might want to ask yourself who will be responsible for any outstanding medical bills and funeral costs. What would happen if your family had to relocate or otherwise change their standard of living once you have died? The assumption of immediate death is necessary to determine the current life insurance needs for a family or individual.

When shopping for life insurance, the best strategy is what? The goal is to allow your dependents to maintain their lifestyle in the event of your demise. You want to have enough face value so that the proceeds of the policy could be conservatively invested to yield enough to cover the loss of your income.

What is the purpose of life insurance? The goal is to allow your dependents to maintain their lifestyle in the event of your demise. You want to have enough face value so that the proceeds of the policy could be conservatively invested to yield enough to cover the loss of your income.

Why should buy a policy with sufficient face value of five to seven time your annual salary? "The answer to this question varies, but most planners say five to seven times your annual salary is normal." Because you never know what is gone to happen, and it is always better to have more than enough and not have enough.

What are the key factors in determining the term of your policy? The number of years you need to keep the policy in force to cover your dependents."

When is the best time to get life insurance? When you have dependents. The purpose of life insurance is to allow your dependents to maintain their lifestyle in the event of your demise.

Natural Things You Need to Know in Order to "Obtain Financial Freedom"

9. **Auto Insurance**

   If you own a vehicle in the United States of America it is mandatory that you have auto insurance

   A. When you apply for insurance, how does the insurance company assess what kind of driver you are your age, your sex, your married status, driving record, and the type of car you have?

   B. **A car that has been totaled, what is the Worth?** When an insurance company says car is declared "totaled" that, means that it is worth less, after the deductible, than the amount it would take to restore it. It is probably time to buy a new car.

   C. **How much bodily injury liability insurance do you need?** State minimums do not come close to covering the cost of a serious accident. You should carry bodily-injury coverage of at least **$100,000 per person**, and **$300,000** per accident, and property-damage coverage of **$50,000**, or a minimum of **$300,000** on a single-limit policy.

   D. **What is the average numbers of years a driver files a claim?** The average driver files a collision claim of some sort once every three years and a comprehensive claim once every ten years.

   E. **What are the indicators that would make your auto insurance cheaper?** A person with a history of responsible driving, in a car that is not likely to get snatched will find cheaper auto insurance than someone who has been in several accidents and drives a car that's popular with thieves.

   F. **When you file a collision claim, what must you do in reference to vehicles parts?** A shop in your insurer's network may fix your car faster, but because the insurance company wants to keep repair costs low, they may skimp on quality.

   G. **What is meant by the term OEM parts?** The original equipment manufacturer).

H. **When a hit-and-run driver strikes your car, what kind of coverage will you need?** Uninsured motorist coverage will cover you if a hit-and-run driver hits your car, if someone who does not have adequate insurance hits your car, or if you are hit as a pedestrian.

I. **What is one of the main reasons that will cause you to be dropped by your insurance company?** Failing to report a teenage driver, Honesty is the best insurance policy. The insurer would probably pay if a teenager, not mentioned on your policy, were in an accident. They would, likely, drop you immediately afterward for dishonesty.

J. **What kind of records can insurers access from your motor vehicle record?** Your motor vehicle record, It makes no sense to lie about your background, because insurers can access all of these.

Natural Things You Need to Know in Order "Obtain Financial Freedom"

10. **Renter Insurance -** The Bottom Line Renter's insurance provides coverage for your personal belongings, whether they are in your home, car or with you while you are on vacation. In addition, renter's insurance provides liability coverage in case someone is injured in your home or if you accidently cause injury to someone.

    ### Six reasons why you should have Renter Insurance:
    One - It is affordable,
    Two - It covers losses to personal property,
    Three - Your property owner might require it,
    Four - It provides liability coverage,
    Five - It covers your belongings when you travel,
    Six - It may cover additional living expenses.

CHAPTER 2 QUESTIONS

Natural Things You Need to Know in Order to "Obtain Financial Freedom"

True and False

1. True ___ or False ___. In order to reach a goal, you must have one.

2. True ___ or False ___. The first thing to getting your spending under control is making a list of things for which you are spending your money.

3. True ___ or False ___. Banks are not your friend, but they are in business to make money by known and unknown fees. Choose your bank carefully.

4. True ___ or False ___. There are two red flags warning that your spending (debts) is out of control. First, when you are making a minimum payment. Second, when your credit cards credit cards are maxed out.

5. True ___ or False ___. Credit cards and Debit cards are not the same.

6. True ___ or False ___. Buying and leasing a car are not the same.

Fill in blank

7. What is the monthly payment you pay for insurance called? _____.

8. Life insurance is need when life end and your family have _____, and _____ expenses.

9. What is mandatory in order to drive a vehicle in the United States of America _____.

10. When renting an apartment, car, or anything of value, what type of insurance should you have? _____.

Section II
Building a Strong Financial House

Things you need to know in Order To "build" A Strong **Financial** House

A strong financial house has each level in order.

In everything in life do it in decency and order.

On a scale of 1 –10, how strong is your financial house?

FIRST LEVEL OF BUILDING A STRONG FINANCIAL HOUSE

GOALS AND DREAMS

- Vacation

- House

- Car

- Own your own Business

- Employer

- Business

- Self Employed

SECOND LEVEL OF BUILDING A STRONG FINANCIAL HOUSE

EMERGENCY ACCOUNT

- **TWELVE TIMES MONTHLY EXPENSES (Married)**

- **SEVEN TIMES MONTHLY EXPENSES (Single)**

- **EMERGENCY ACCOUNT**

(Example: tires blow out, appliances breakdown, family member dies, and shopping is not an emergency).

THIRD LEVEL OF BUILDING A STRONG FINANCIAL HOUSE

PROTECTION MANAGEMENT

1. Health Insurance

2. Life Insurance

3. Auto Insurance

4. Homeowners Insurance

5. Long Term care

6. Legal Services

FORTH LEVEL OF BUILDING A STRONG FINANCIAL HOUSE
BUDGETING
What is the difference between expenses and debts?

Monthly Income		Monthly Expenses	
Your Pay	$	Rent or Mortgage	$
Spouse's Pay	$	Utilities (Phone, Gas, Electric, cable, etc.)	$
Bonuses	$	Insurance (home, auto, life, health, etc.)	$
Commissions	$	Food	$
Tips	$	Incidental Home (paper products, non-food items, etc.)	$
Interest Received	$	Clothing	$
Investment Earnings	$	Auto (gas, tolls, maintenance)	$
Rental Income	$	Debt Payments (auto, credit cards, store cards, etc.)	$
Pension Income	$	Child Care	$
Social Security Income	$	Health (medical, dental, eye, etc./not covered by insurance)	$
Alimony Received	$	Taxes (not taken out of paycheck)	$
Child Support Received	$	Gifts (charities, church, holidays, birthdays, etc.)	$
Other Income	$	Entertainment (movies, vacation, videos, etc.)	$
	$	Personal Allowances	$
	$	Other Expenses	$
Totals	$		$

Please Note as a Suggestion!
1. 10% - Tithing.
2. 10% - Sowing Seeds 10% (Sow a seed to meet a need).
3. 10% - Personal Saving 10% (learning to pay yourself).
4. 70% - Make the necessary adjustment to live off 70%.

FIFTH LEVEL OF BUILDING A STRONG FINANCIAL HOUSE

DEBT MANAGEMENT

- **Debt Consolidation**

    N/A homeowner

    Debt stacking

    Financial analysis

- **Debt Elimination**

    - Homeowner

    - Eliminate all debt outside the mortgage

    - Biweekly payment (reduce your mortgage)

SIXTH LEVEL OF BUILDING A STRONG FINANCIAL HOUSE

EDUCATION / RETIREMENT

College funds

529 college saving plan / in connecting with upromise.com. A 529 Plan is an education savings plan operated by a state or educational institution designed to help families set aside funds for future college costs. It is named after Section 529 of the Internal Revenue Code, which created these types of savings plans in 1996.

Simplified tax reporting

- Contributions to a 529 plan do not have to be reported on your federal tax return.
- You will not receive a Form 1099 to report taxable or nontaxable earnings until the year you make withdrawals.
- Deposits to a 529 plan up to $14,000 per individual per year ($28,000 for married couples filing jointly) will qualify for the annual **gift tax exclusion**.

Retirement (Please NOTE, the date that YOU start working is the day YOU start saving for RETIREMENT)

Roth IRA –tax deferred / tax-free if you keep for 5 years maximum amount per year $4,000.00 per person. Eliminate all debts outside of the mortgage biweekly payment cannot touch until 59.5 years old or tax penalty

SEVENTH LEVEL OF BUILDING A STRONG FINANCIAL HOUSE

REVIEW LEVELS 1-6

1. Goals and Dreams
2. Income Protection \ Emergency Accounts
3. Protection Management
4. Household Budgeting
5. Debt Management
6. Children Education / Your Retirement

RULE of 72

Take any interest rate and divided it into the number 72 and that approximates how long it will take your money to double.

Amount in Investment

(1) 4% double every 18 years - (2) 6% double every 12 years - (3)12% double every 6 years

Numbers of years	4%	6%	12%
0	$10,000	$10,000	$10,000
6	----------	----------	$20,000
12	----------	$20,000	$40,000
18	$20,000	----------	$80,000
24	----------	$40,000	$160,000
30	----------	----------	$320,000
36	$40,000	$80,000	$640,000
Numbers of years	4%	6%	12%
0	$10,000	$10,000	$10,000
6	----------	----------	$20,000
12	----------	$20,000	$40,000
18	$20,000	----------	$80,000
24	----------	$40,000	$160,000
30	----------	----------	$320,000
36	$40,000	$80,000	$640,000

What age do you think you will stop working _____?

D -death **D** -debt (outside of our mortgage) **I** -Income Replacement **M**-Mortgage **E** -Education

Section III
The **_Spiritual things_** you need to know in Order To "Build" A Strong **Financial House, and** "How to obtain Financial Freedom"

Chapter 3
There Are Two Kingdoms on Planet Earth!

The "world's population is over 7 billion" (1) and it is estimated that only one third of its population has heard the Gospel of the Kingdom of God. For this reason, there is still an enormous amount of work to be done to proclaim the saving knowledge of Jesus Christ to the world. The gospel is free to all, and yet the process of evangelism requires a significant amount of money. Missionaries need funds to travel, along with supplies and provision for their work; church congregations need facilities to accommodate the people in their communities. The list is endless as to the many ways we can reach our world with the gospel. In short, money is needed in order to evangelize the world and if there were ever a time in which the church needed money, it is now!

I have been a Christian for over 25 years, during which I have always desired to evangelize and expand the Kingdom of God on this earth. Over the years, I have become frustrated whenever I see sincere people of God with a heart to win their community for Jesus hampered by not having what is needed to accomplish this task. For instance, a while ago I knew a pastor who genuinely loved the Lord and was seeking to expand his ministry in his community by purchasing a building with 10 acres of land. I believe God desired this church to have that property to better meet the needs of their community and expand God's work in that area. The pastor and his congregation stood in agreement and believed God for the property. The pastor attempted to procure financing through several banks, but to no avail. Disappointingly, he was unable to purchase the property and it became investment property for "the world".

Having witnessed several situations similar to this one, I have come to understand that countless sincere people of God do not understand how to use biblically correct methods for obtaining revenue to carry out God's mission and build up His Kingdom on this earth. Many churches are experiencing financial pressures that cause them to seek out other means of financial increase. There are churches that have to sponsor dinner sales, car washes, shopping trips, and other projects of this nature to raise money for the purpose of carrying out God's mission, or simply to pay normal operating expenses, i.e. monthly utility bills, building maintenance, and salaries. Unfortunately, in many of these churches it is easy to find people who only put a dollar or two in the collection basket because they do not understand biblical tithing and offering.

While the churches of the living God are often struggling, you will see new construction projects such as shopping centers, business parks, etc. in many cities all along their streets and highways. I often say to myself, "all that construction requires money". There just does not seem to be a shortage of money for new construction projects for "the world" but where is the money for fulfilling the mission of God?

Understanding Kingdom Principles

In order to answer the question, where is the money for fulfilling the mission of God? We have to go back to the beginning! This question is answered by understanding the relationship of God with mankind and mankind with creation.

Two Kingdoms on One Planet
    1) Kingdom of God - (Matthews 4:17), Operative Economic Principle (Giving and Receiving)

    2) Kingdom of darkness- (Matthews 12:26), Operative Economic Principle (Buying and Selling –Hook or Crook)

When God created Adam, He gave him authority over the earth, making him ruler over the earth. Genesis 1:26-31, this was the establishment of the Kingdom of God on earth. Adam caused the fall of man when he chose to disobey God and eat from the tree of the knowledge of good and evil. By choosing to disobey, Adam lost his government and handed it over to the serpent, the prince or ruler of darkness, who is satan* (*in this book lowercase will be used to denote "satan" except at the beginning of sentences). Satan's goal was not merely to tempt Adam to disobey God, but rather to take over the territory (the earth) that belonged to Adam, including Adam's authority. When Adam disobeyed, he abdicated his authority and became subject to satan's authority. Satan now ruled the earth. However, all was not lost. In *Genesis 3:15*, God made a promise to send a seed to crush the head of satan and restore the kingdom authority back to man. The seed to which He referred was Jesus.

God sent Jesus to restore Heaven's government and rulership back on earth through man. This created two kingdoms on earth, the Kingdom of God and the kingdom of darkness.

Before Jesus came, the kingdom that existed on earth was the kingdom of darkness. The Kingdom of God was the first kingdom on earth through Adam, but Adam lost it to satan.

Even though Jesus came to restore the Kingdom of Heaven's rule back to man, He did not wipe out or destroy the kingdom of darkness. Instead, according to *Matthew 4:17,* Jesus stood up in the middle of the kingdom of darkness and announced that the Kingdom of Heaven had arrived! Jesus did not destroy the kingdom of darkness when he brought back the rulership of the Kingdom of Heaven to the earth. Therefore, today, we have two kingdoms on planet earth. So, you are either in the Kingdom of Heaven or you are in the kingdom of darkness. It is that simple.

To clarify, the Kingdom of God is not a religion. In fact, true Christianity is not a religion either- it means that we are supposed to be Christ-like; conducting ourselves as citizens of God's kingdom. Christianity is not about religion, but rather, it is about citizenship.

Jesus understood that there are two kingdoms or governments operating on earth. In *Matthew 12:22-29* when Jesus cast out a demon, the religious people accused Him of casting out demons by the power of demons. Jesus asked them, "Can satan can cast out satan?" Then Jesus explained that if any kingdom is divided against itself, it cannot stand, so he could not be working for satan while destroying satan.

Jesus told them that he cast out demons by the power and the finger of God, **"know this: that the kingdom of heaven is come upon you."** In other words, he was explaining how you cannot operate from both kingdoms, while also declaring that the Kingdom of God had arrived. Just as Jesus understood this, we need to understand that what is going on in the earth is not about people or money, it is about kingdoms and how they govern. It is about the Kingdom of God verses the kingdom of darkness. Which kingdom are you in? Never compare a religion to the Kingdom of God or reduce the Kingdom of God to a religion. Jesus' assignment was to bring God's kingdom back to the earth.

God's goal was never religion, but to rule the earth through a relationship with his rulers, his people, through the Holy Spirit. God is a Spirit and He created spiritual children out of his own spirit, and he put them in a dirt body on the earth. We have a spirit being living in a physical (dirt) body.

Once someone enters into relationship with Jesus Christ through salvation, and the Holy Spirit takes residence in this person, he or she is now capable of operating in the Kingdom of Heaven on this earth.

The key to the government of heaven ruling the earth is that the Holy Spirit is in touch with the spirit of the person that is residing in their body, and then the body carries out heaven's wishes. Again, the Holy Spirit communicates the instructions that are in the mind of God to man's spirit, so that man can rule the earth and bring the government of heaven to the earth.

In short, the earth receives the influence of the unseen kingdoms through humankind. Interestingly, the devil's kingdom and God's kingdom must operate through man on this earth. The devil desires to make earth a literal "hell on earth." Contrariwise, God's plan has always been to bring heaven to earth. This is depicted in "The Lord's Prayer".

Remember when Jesus was asked by His disciples to teach them how to pray? Jesus agreed, instructing them to pray this way *'Our Father which art in Heaven'*. Jesus put this first to make sure you address the right government, the Kingdom of Heaven. You're accessing the Kingdom of Heaven, but you are addressing God himself, so remember that you've got to respect him. Therefore, the next part says, 'Hollowed be thy name'. We know that there is power in the name of the Lord, but here Jesus is instructing us to hallow His name. "Hallow" means you are recognizing that God is a God of integrity; you know that He keeps His word; He is pure in motive; He never lies and He keeps His promises.

Next, He says, 'Thy kingdom come' and this is where you make your request. These requests are not from an outsider looking in, hoping for some great being in the sky to hear you and help you. Your requests are based on your rights as a citizen in the Kingdom of God! Remember, that as a citizen, you are entitled to food, clothing, and everything else. So, on a larger scale, we desire to see Heaven here on earth. Jesus said to pray, 'Thy will be done on earth as it is in Heaven.'

This is where it gets really exciting! The challenge may be initially in discovering where God's will is, but finding God's will is fairly simple. God has His divine plans in His mind; plans of what He wants to bring to pass on this earth, yet, He desires that we ask Him to do it through us! What a privilege to be citizens of Heaven while on earth, establishing Heaven on earth through His direction, and then receiving His reward for doing His will.

As mentioned before, God reveals His will through the Holy Spirit to man, and then His will is carried out by a man who is conducting himself as a citizen of the Kingdom of Heaven ('Thy will be done on earth as it is in heaven').

In order for us to understand what it means to be citizens of Heaven and for God's will to be done on earth as it is in Heaven, we have to remember that Heaven is a real place. Heaven is a real place with a government; it has laws, boundaries, territories, and citizenships; it has the execution of justice, rights, and privileges.

The Bible teaches that heaven is a country. It has a governing authority; it has a seat of power, which is the throne of God; it has servants called angels; it has an environment that is maintained by God, where there is light at all times and absolutely no darkness. Heaven is a powerfully awesome place. The kingdom of Heaven is not a religion, but a government with a country, and a territory within that country that operates by governing laws and principles. Citizenship is required for your own entrance into the Kingdom of Heaven. In natural terms, we understand that if you are not a citizen of a country, you are either a visitor, an ambassador, or you are an illegal occupant. Whether a citizen, visitor, ambassador, etc. You are required to learn and live by the laws of that country. Similarly, to become a citizen of Heaven you first have to learn and live by the laws established by God.

In order to become a citizen of the Kingdom of Heaven, you obey the "constitution" or the terms of the Holy Bible for citizenship. The bible says in *John 3;* that *"you must be born again."* to enter the Kingdom of Heaven.

The process of being born again is outlined in several scriptures, including *Romans 10:8-9* *"That if thou shalt confess with thy mouth the Lord Jesus, and believe in thine heart that God hath raised Him from the dead, thou shalt be saved."*

Once you become a citizen of Heaven, you need to read the constitution (the Bible) which explains the government of Heaven's responsibility for your protection and welfare. Without becoming familiar with the constitution of Heaven you leave yourself vulnerable for satan to take advantage of your lack of knowledge of your own rights as a citizen. That is why satan is called the prince of darkness. His number one objective is to keep you in darkness, or maintain your ignorance, of the Kingdom of God.

The devil knows that once you read and study the Bible, the constitution of Heaven, you will gain the knowledge and power to apply God's Word on this earth. The Holy Spirit is the author of the Bible (constitution); He is your lawyer, your counselor and the one that has been sent to help you understand the constitution, leading you into and teaching you all the complicated truths.

The laws that are in the Bible can also be referred to as "keys". When Jesus said that I give unto you the "keys to the kingdom" in *Matthew 16:13-19*, He was talking about learning the laws and the principles by which the Kingdom of Heaven operates, "Keys" of the kingdom are the laws of the kingdom, and the laws are rooted in spiritual and natural principles.

Isaiah 9:6-7; states that Jesus came to bring the government of Heaven back to mankind. *Matthew 4:17* illustrates that Jesus' arrival also proclaimed the arrival of the kingdom of God, and His first public statement was that the kingdom of Heaven had arrived. In other words, the Bible is declaring that Jesus will teach you the principles by which the kingdom of Heaven operates, even the secrets of the Kingdom. Jesus said in *Matthew 13:11* and *Luke 8:10* that it has been given to us to know the mysteries (secrets) of the Kingdom of Heaven.

Jesus said I give unto you the keys, the operation of the Kingdom of Heaven, and I will reveal to you the mysteries of the Kingdom of Heaven. As stated earlier, you must be born again spiritually to get *into* the kingdom, but once you are in the Kingdom of Heaven, you need to know how to *live* in the kingdom of Heaven, hence, the keys. You can have the title to your car, but you will not be able to get in and drive it unless you have the keys that match your door and the ignition! To operate in the Kingdom of Heaven, you must know where your keys are and how to use them. You must learn God's laws, principles, precepts, judgments, and statutes. Statutes are fixed and predictable principles, meaning, you can predict the result.

Psalm 119:1-7 describes the word of God as being like a statute. Based on our definition of statute, we can be sure that the Bible has fixed and predictable principles. Therefore, if the word of God says that giving is a statute, you do not have to worry about it. For instance, *Luke 6:38* is a statute; you can predict what is going to happen if you activate it. **Please see Appendix A.**

"You must understand the difference between the two systems, and be willing to change. Recognize that the old system is not getting the job done, and spiritually separate yourself from the old system of finance and get in the new way of living." (Thompson, 2003, Pg.125)

Chapter 3 – Questions – Two Kingdoms

True or False:

1. True ___ or False ___. There two kingdoms on planet earth.

2. True ___ or False ___. God's Kingdom was on planet earth first.

3. True ___ or False ___. Adam lost his God given dominion and authority on earth.

4. True ___ or False ___. The kingdom of darkness was established on planet earth because of Adam disobedience?

Fill in the blank

5. Jesus came to restore what on earth, according to (Matthew 4:17) _____.

6. Based upon Isaiah 9:6-7, Jesus brought what back to the earth _____.

7. Based upon Matthew 4:17, what did Jesus announce was at hand? _____.

8. Based upon Matthew 16:13-19, what did Jesus say He will give us _____.

9. What are the two kingdom on planet earth? the _____, and the _____.

Multiple Choice

10. The Kingdom of God operate by the principle of
    A) Giving and receiving
    B) Buying and selling
    C) Hook or Crook
    D) Sealing and selling
    E) All of the Above

    ANSWER): _____

Chapter 4
The Master Plan of God and the Glory Team

The Master Plan- God wants to open up the whole realm of His nature and put it on display. It says in ***Deuteronomy 8:18 (KJV)*** *"But thou shalt remember the Lord thy God: for it is he that giveth thee power to get wealth, that he may establish his covenant which he sware unto thy fathers, as it is this day."* If God gave us power to get wealth, it must be because He has a plan.

Some people forget that God is as smart as He is. God never releases anything nor does He let it be revealed without having His own reasons - He has a master plan. His plan is to send people into every part of the world so He can receive glory. When God sends us out, it's not about our careers or the subject of our creation. It is, however, about God's expectation of our impact on society resulting in His love and grace being shown to individuals who would not find Him any other way; but to accomplish this in the earthly realm, you need money. Salvation is free to mankind, but it cost God His Son and it costs to get the gospel to the world.

As we approach the subject of how to obtain financial freedom, I am reminded of the Olympic Games and how each nation came up with the concept of what they call the "Dream Team", especially in the areas of basketball, volleyball, and swimming. During the Olympic Games held this year of 2008, the United States sent a team of basketball players that we called our "Redeem Team" because of previous losses. They were able to go on and win the gold medal for the United States.

This is similar in comparison with the Kingdom of God versus the kingdom of darkness. We have the Glory Team representing the Kingdom of God which consists of the ***Holy Spirit, the Holy Angels, the Rhema, the Seed and Solid (good) Ground.*** To be more specific, we have the ***Angel*** who is the Minister of Finance for the Kingdom of God, the ***Rhema Word of God*** and the saints of God who are led by the ***Holy Spirit*** to sow the ***Seeds*** in ***Solid Ground*** which will produce a great harvest in a short period of time. For example, what would normally take five years can be done within six months to one year and this will assist in expanding of Kingdom of God.

1. The Holy Spirit: The third person of the Godhead. "The Holy Spirit is going to take dominion over finances so that Jesus can inherit His reward. There is going to be a commissioning next year of the five-fold ministry to the world, not just in the church- prophets in the entertainment industry, apostles in the government, and evangelists in the business realm. God is breathing on the five-fold to display his manifold wisdom." *(Retrieved 2008, Sept. 5, P.1.)* *(www.kingdomfinanceseminar.com/welcomeminister.ph)*

This is nothing for us as believers because the scriptures tell us that when Israel was delivered from Egyptian captivity, all of the wealth of Egypt was transferred into the hands of the Israelites in one day because God caused them to have favor *(**Exodus 3:21, 12:35**)*. This concept is further confirmed in ***Proverbs 13:22*** *"A good man leaveth an inheritance to his children's children: and the wealth of the sinner is laid up for the just."*

2. The Ministering Angel of Finance and two worshipping angels: Within in the United States government, we have various leaders over various departments.

The same is true within the Kingdom of God; there are angels that oversee certain areas. Michael the Archangel oversees the nation of Israel. *"**The Angel who is The Minister of Finance of the Kingdom is being released along with resource angels to invest Jesus' kingdom money to bring forth His inheritance on the Earth.**" (Retrieved 2008, Sept. 5, P.1.)* *(www.kingdomfinanceseminar.com/welcomeminister.ph)*

3. Rhema: Rhema is the spoken word. The words *logos* and *rhema* have both been translated as the same word in most versions of the Bible and it has confused those outside of prophetic congregations. Rhema is the spoken word of God and denotes the teaching or utterances of God's words through someone declaring the mind of God. Rhema is the divine instruction by preachers of the gospel, words of prophecy and prophetic announcement.

God still speaks to those with the faith to be able to hear His voice. The Word of God consists of that which is written in the Bible and the Rhema word which is the same spiritual word from God that was given to the prophets of old and recorded in the Bible.

Studying from the Bible is the best way to learn about the things of God. But if the Bible is elevated to legalistic rules and regulations to follow beyond what the Holy Spirit teaches, it becomes according to the letter and is the same Pharisee spirit that Jesus came to deliver us from. The Bible itself cannot save you; only Jesus can save you. Rhema is the Word meditated on by the spirit through the study of the written word. It is the revelation given to us by God to help us understand and it is the prophetic articulation of that revelation.

   4.   *Seed sown into good ground*:   As we are learning how to obtain financial freedom, it is the Rhema word of God that is spoken to us as we prepare to sow. Again, we have the logos (written word), but we need the Rhema (spoken) word of God to receive direction on what good ground to sow our seed into so that we can reap the harvest that God would have us to reap. More detail on this topic will be shared in Chapter Six which explains the Law of Seedtime and Harvest.

   5.   *The process of seed sown into good ground*: A farmer would scatter his seed in his field so that the seeds would produce the respective fruit (along with more seeds) and after a time the crop would be reaped and then harvested. *Matthew 13:3 and Luke 8:5* both mark the beginning of the parable of the sower and the seed. The farmer scattered his seed in his field. We learn from the Gospel of Mark (*Mark 4:1-8*) that the seed is the word of God and the field is the world. Therefore, the word of God is sown in the world to produce fruit. Bad seeds can be sown along with the good seeds producing undesirable fruit. However, God knows the difference between what His seed produces and what the undesirable seed produces. By implication we see that a seed will grow whether it is good (desirable) or bad (undesirable).

"But this I say, He which soweth sparingly shall reap also sparingly; and he which soweth bountifully shall reap also bountifully." ***2 Corinthians 9:6(KJV)***

Paul states that what you reap will be dependent upon your what you sow. The more you sow, the more you will reap so that you will have even more to sow. This appears to be a spiritual principle that opens the door for God to supply what you need and to bless you with abundance. Other insights to this principle are:

- ***(Proverbs 11:24-25 NIV)*** *One man gives freely, yet gains even more; another withholds unduly, but comes to poverty. A generous man will prosper; he who refreshes others will himself be refreshed.*

- ***(Proverbs 19:17 NIV)*** *He who is kind to the poor lends to the LORD, and he will reward him for what he has done.*

The key point here is that God will give you increase as long as you give. The fact that God will ensure that your needs are met and that you will have plenty to give away brings up an interesting question about sowing.

What is proper sowing? What gifts are considered sowing seed that will guarantee provisions from God? According to the scriptures that we have examined regarding this principle, it is clear that meeting someone's need is considered valid sowing. For example, a birthday or Christmas presents are not sowing seed. However, giving clothes and or money to someone in need is considered valid sowing. Additionally, valid sowing must be accompanied by proper motive. Sowing to get is not valid sowing; sowing to help is valid sowing. Sow to bless and then you will receive. Do not sow to receive thinking you will be blessed. God's law doesn't work that way.

Sowing Method- Paul indicates that sowing or giving must be done with purpose. We have to decide what we want to give and we must do it cheerfully. Giving out of compulsion or obligation is not pleasing to God and I would dare say that it does not produce a harvest according to the principle of sowing and reaping.

Your giving is from the heart and is to meet the needs of someone, to support your church because you believe in its ministry or at the commandment of God for a specific purpose. Sowing in this manner will produce provisions for you and provide you with more that is available to give away. The proper method of sowing is to sow from the motivations of your godly heart and to do so willingly and cheerfully.

Benefits of This Principle - You do not have to be afraid to give if you operate in this principle. Remember that your giving is done from that which you are able to give and not necessarily sacrificially (though you may sacrifice to give sometimes).

By faith you know that God is true to His Word and you do not have to worry about lack or be afraid to give to someone in need. The Bible says *"He who is kind to the poor lends to the LORD, and he will reward him for what he has done."* **(Proverbs 19:17 NIV)** The law of sowing and reaping frees us to use our resources to help others without anxiety over a possible lack of provision for future needs.

"Do not be anxious about anything, but in everything, by prayer and petition, with thanksgiving, present your requests to God." **(Phil 4:6 NIV)** God will ensure that your needs are met and that you have plenty to give to others if you sow.

The motive of giving is also a determinant of what is harvested. Whatever we sow is what we will reap. It becomes important to check our motives to ensure that we are sowing the seeds that we want to sow.

Chapter 4 - Questions – *The Master Plan*

True or False

1. True ___ or False ___. God has a master plan for financing the Kingdom of God on earth.

2. True ___ or False ___. God has a glory Team working on His behalf in the earth to finances His Kingdom.

3. True ___ or False ___. The Holy Spirit is a member of the Glory Team.

4. True ___ or False ___. There Angels who serves as finance ministers.

5. True ___ or False ___. There are two primary means or ways of receiving from God, the Logos Word, and the *Rhema Word.*

Fill in the blank

6. Who is the Holy Spirit? _____.

7. What is Seed sown into good ground? _____.

8. What is proper sowing? _____.

9. What is the proper Sowing Method? _____.

Multiple Choices

10. The Kingdom of God operate by the principle of:

    A) The Holy Spirit
    B) The Ministering Angel of Finance
    C) Rhema
    D) Seed sown into good ground:
    E) The law of Seed time and harvest time
    F) All the above

    ANSWER): _____

Chapter 5
Stewardship and the Kingdom of God

The lack of understanding of stewardship is a discipleship issue. This issue is exacerbated because stewardship is also a silent subject—we do not talk about it in church! Seminaries do not teach it, pastors do not preach it, churches do not plan for it and people do not talk about it, Jesus did!

In *Mark 1:15*, Jesus entreats us to leave the world behind and come under God's reign. He taught that the Kingdom of God was "at hand," and that we should change our lives. We need to release control, let Jesus be Lord of all--life, abilities, money, and other resources-- in order to serve our new master. In *Matthew 4:17*, we read *"Repent, for the kingdom of heaven is near."* Repentance means to change one's mind or purpose, including the acknowledgment of God's lordship in every area of our lives. This has specific consequences in the administration of our resources. Since God will one day hold us accountable for what we did with what He gave us, church leaders are responsible to make sure the people obey God with what they are given. We must help them become faithful stewards.

This gift was distinguished by the change in a man's heart. God's presence through the infilling of the Holy Spirit helped him abandon his idols and turn to pure devotion to Jesus. God's gift made him rich in eternal things although he was poor in earthly treasures. The result of God's grace was an intense desire both to tell and to give. He did not just talk about God's grace he lived it. People who understand what they have in the Kingdom of our Lord give generously and joyfully. This conviction is the starting point for proper stewardship of all that we possess.

Webster's New Collegiate Dictionary defines a steward as "one employed in a large household or estate to manage domestic concerns (as the supervision of servants, collection of rents and keeping of accounts)." In short, a steward is one who takes care of someone else's property.

- *Old Testament reference*: those "over the household"
- *New Testament reference*: "managers or stewards"

Perhaps the most vivid biblical story illustrating stewardship is Joseph, the manager of Potiphar's house (*Genesis 39:4-5*). The volume of biblical teaching on stewardship (over 2350 verses) demands that we pursue an understanding of the term to a deeper level.

The Hebrew concept of stewardship begins and ends with God. Adam and Eve were given dominion to "rule on His behalf" over His creation in the garden. Clearly, God did not give up his ownership (even before man's fall) and later, His covenant people were given specific responsibilities in regards to His resources (redemption of Firstfruits for example). In *Deuteronomy 25:19*, we are taught to be good stewards of the land and resources God has given us, but God's sovereignty is unquestionable. Scripture contains a host of explicit instructions for caring for the land.

The idea behind the Year of Jubilee (every 50th year when debts are forgiven and land reverts to the original owners) underlines the fact that all the land rightfully belonged to Him (*Leviticus 25:23*). Even Israel's songs of worship reinforced these principles. "The earth is the Lord's and everything in it, the world, and all who live in it; for he founded it. . . " (*Psalm 24:1, 2*)

The theology of God's ownership also under girds the practice of tithes and offerings whose core purpose was the worship of God—acknowledging Him as owner and giver of all things. David's prayer in *2 Chronicles 29:14-18* ties our giving to God's ownership.

The Old Testament teaching on stewardship may be summarized in three principles:

- God is the owner of everything
- God's covenant people are responsible for their management of His resources
- Giving is a worshipful response to God's ownership of all things.

1. *Good stewardship begins with the recognition that God is the owner of all things*. "Everything comes from you" (*1 Chronicles 29:14 The Message Bible*). It is impossible to "give ourselves or our things to God" because He already owns them. We can only recognize and submit to His ownership.

2. *As stewards we are entrusted with goods to care for as part of kingdom discipleship until the return of the master, Jesus Christ.* The parable of the talents (*Matthew 25:14-20, Luke 19:12-27*) shows that servants receive different gifts according to their abilities.

   God gives us only what we can aptly handle. He expects an increase, and He expects us to bear fruit in His kingdom. His main concern is that we be faithful with what we have been given.

3. *Earthly resources can be used for eternal purposes.* In Jesus' parable of the shrewd manager (*Luke 16*), the key lesson is that earthly wealth can create eternal value. Jesus warns that money can control our lives (*Luke 16:13*) as it had for the Pharisees (*Luke 16:14*). We are to view money as a tool God can use to accomplish eternal purposes. Wise stewards reap an eternal reward (*Luke 16:9*).

4. *Our stewardship must not serve our own purposes*, but the purpose of the master, Jesus Christ. The third servant in the parable of the talents did what was right in his own eyes and was judged harshly for not obeying the will of the master. Obedience, however, is the minimum standard, with no special reward.

5. *As stewards we need a balanced picture of hardship.* Most Americans experience ongoing lifestyle inflation. Each year the bar is raised, yesterday's wants become today's needs. This can distort our view of hardship. In fact, God often calls His people to endure hardship. (*Matthew 8:19-22, 10:22, Mark 10:45*) A balanced view means that God's call on our lives should not be filtered by what is most comfortable or most difficult. Minimizing debt and giving sacrificially may require a simpler lifestyle--some would find this easy, others a hardship. In most cases, the "hardship" associated with obeying God's will is justified.

6. *We will be held accountable for our stewardship.* All three "stewardship" parables feature a moment of reckoning. The unjust steward is fired. The faithful and unfaithful stewards are rewarded and punished respectively. Although salvation is a free gift by God's grace (*Ephesians 2:8, 9*), each of us will face judgment to determine the rewards for how we have lived. Redemption does not remove accountability. (*Romans 14:12*)

7. ***Our stewardship embraces the spiritual and the material.*** We have already mentioned stewardship of the church, the gospel, and spiritual gifts. The use of time and opportunities to minister (***Ephesians 5:15, 16***), care of our physical bodies as temples of the Holy Spirit (***1 Corinthians 6:19***), and hospitality to others in our homes (***Hebrews 13:2, 1 Peter 4:9***) also fall under our stewardship responsibilities.

Christians must learn to employ the weapons of spiritual warfare not just in extraordinary situations involving the occult or demonic manifestations, but also in the ordinary world of earning wages, paying bills and tithing. A lifestyle characterized by stewardship is a spiritual battle that must be won. Spiritual warfare must be considered as a cause for Christian resistance to biblical stewardship along with the more obvious — ignorance and hard-heartedness.

This is evidenced in ***Matthew 6:19-24*** which contains a strongly worded passage that one cannot serve two masters. God and money are diametrically opposed in a struggle for the hearts of believers. The "slave" imagery used is a clue that Jesus viewed allegiance to money as a form of spiritual bondage. A widely accepted method of spiritual warfare is to operate in the spirit opposite of what is being manifested as illustrated in ***Proverbs 15:1***, which reads, "A gentle answer turns away wrath."

When anger is present, respond in gentleness; when a spirit of pride takes over, nothing will expose it better than the spirit of humility. When there is greed, let generosity abound. When materialism calls for lifestyle inflation, let the Christian live simply, with a generous heart furthering godly purposes.

The example of Jesus, who freely gave of Himself and laid aside His rights and privileges that we might have freedom, is a worthy goal.
(***2 Corinthians 8:9, Philippians 2:6, 7***) We serve a generous God, so let us be generous people.

Our discussion of what I refer to as "Health and Wealth Prosperity Gospel" includes both a correction and a direction. Our correction in this area is to avoid a judgmental attitude, focusing instead on speaking God's truth.

First, we reject as unbiblical the suggestion that although God has set up universal laws of prosperity that govern the universe—we are to somehow put them into operation by faith and positive confession (name it and claim it).

Second, we must reject as unbiblical the claim that God wants to meet not only the believer's every need but to grant every desire as well. Finally, we must reject as unbiblical the claim that although Jesus died to redeem man from poverty, a believer who is poor has dishonored God by failing to appropriate this specific deliverance.

Clearly, scripture shows God's desire to bless and even prosper His children, e.g. Abraham (***Genesis 13:2, 6***), Isaac (***Genesis 26:13,14***) and Jacob (***Genesis 32:9-12***). Paul's letter to Timothy warns against unwise use of riches, but affirms God's provision "who richly provides us with everything for our enjoyment" **(*1 Timothy 6:17 NIV*)**. God's desire to bless is balanced by warnings regarding riches. Jesus condemned the rich fool in ***Luke 12:13-20*** and said it was hard for a rich man to enter the Kingdom of God (***Luke 18:24, 25***).

A balanced view affirms that wealth is not evil in and of itself, but it is our attitude towards wealth, namely our desire for it, that can produce evil **(*1 Timothy 6:9,10*)**.

The primary error of the prosperity movement is its distortion of biblical principles concerning God's provision.

God is not dishonored by believers who have little or no possessions (***Luke 6:20, James 2:5, 1 Corinthians 4:11***) Also, it is clearly not God's desire that any lack what they need. Material poverty is part of the curse of our fallen world—much like sickness or disease. However, we do see in scripture a connection between faithful stewardship and material blessing, but it is one of general principle rather than specific promise. ***Haggai 1:6-12*** illustrates the result of neglecting God's purposes in our stewardship.

Malachi proclaimed that the people of Israel, during the Persian period, were under the curse of God for robbing Him of His tithes and offerings. He then reminds them of God's promise, *"Bring the whole tithe into the storehouse, that there may be food in my house. Test me in this . . . And see if I will not throw open the floodgates of heaven and pour out so much blessing that you will not have room enough for it"* **(*Malachi 3:10 NIV*)**.

Our contention is that if the church embraces the reign and rule of God in the management of all its possessions, then it will see, as a by-product of the advancement of the Kingdom, a powerful liberation of God's people. In America, we need to relearn the lesson of *Luke 12:48*.

Although Christians disagree over the place of the tithe in today's lifestyle, it has always symbolized the whole—a token which affirms that the whole belongs to God. You cannot read about Abram's giving a tenth of his military spoils to Melchizedek (*Genesis 14:20*) without seeing his no-strings-attached giving which sprang from a heart aligned with God.

Mosaic Law describes various "tithes" (*Numbers 18:21-24; Deuteronomy 12:6,7; 14:22-29*), but God's ultimate desire was for our heart to be aligned with His. *Deuteronomy 14:23NIV* says the purpose of the tithe was "so that you may learn to revere the Lord your God always." Giving the first and best of their earnings was an ongoing reminder that ALL they had belonged to God.

The tithe was never to be "performed" in obligation, but offered in worship as an expression of a grace-birthed heart relationship with God. The spirit of the tithe was always more important to God than the letter.
In *Matthew 23:23 NIV* Jesus affirms the tithe, but rebukes the Pharisees for losing the spirit behind it: "You give a tenth of your spices . . .but you have neglected . . .justice, mercy, and faithfulness. You should have practiced the latter, without neglecting the former."

On the subject of giving, the New Testament does not call for a strict ten percent tithe. Rather, proportional giving, sacrificial giving, and giving based on need are encouraged of those with hearts sold out to God. If, after all, we are merely stewards of what is ultimately owned by God, then the driving question on this issue is not "How much do I give? "How much dare I keep?"

1. **Give First:** The tithe reminds us that God comes first in our lives, He alone deserves preeminence. (*Luke 6:38; Proverbs 3:9, 10*). Tithing is a test of stewardship.

2. **Give Cheerfully:** Focusing on the eternal impact will encourage cheerful giving. "Each man should give what he has decided in his heart to give, not reluctantly or under compulsion, for God loves a cheerful giver." (*2 Corinthians 9:7 NIV*)

3. **Give Faithfully:** Reliability (faithfulness) in giving is the heart of biblical stewardship and, sadly, in short supply in the church today. Christians should live their lives in a way that will result in the Lord saying, "Well done, good and faithful servant" (*Matthew 25:21-23NIV*)

4. **Give Wisely:** Where we give our tithe and offerings is an investment and should be given with wisdom. Give first to your home church (where you are being fed spiritually) then give where you see Kingdom investments multiplying and producing fruit. (*1 Corinthians 9:11*)

5. **Give without Seeking Recognition:** Giving privately guards against religious pride and builds faith into our lives. If our confidence is in God, we will give without anyone else knowing and be content.

Stewardship is the foundation of the larger context of Christian discipleship. Beginning with a wholehearted commitment, let us rekindle our passion for serving Him as true stewards—handling life, money, spiritual gifts, and the gospel message faithfully. Through the power of the Holy Spirit, let us seek to be and to raise godly stewards in our congregations. May God give us the courage to see these issues through Kingdom lenses, to go against the grain of our culture, and raise up the next generation of stewards for God's Kingdom.

Chapter 5 Questions – "Stewardship"

True or False

1. True ___ or False ___. As stewards, we are entrusted with God's goods based upon Matthew 25:14-20, Luke 19:12-27.

2. True ___ or False ___. We will be held accountable for our stewardship.

3. True ___ or False ___. Tithing is a test of stewardship.

4. True ___ or False ___. Your earthly resources can be used for eternal purposes.

5. True ___ or False ___. Our stewardship embraces spiritual things and material things.

Fill in the blank

6. God is the owner of _____ according to Psalm 24:1.

7. God's covenant people are responsible for being _____ over their of God giving resources.

8. Giving is a _____ response to God's ownership of all things.

9. Stewardship is the _____ of the larger context of Christian discipleship.

Multiple Choice

10. How must we give? According to second Corinthians 8:9,

    A) Give First
    B) Give Cheerfully
    C) Give Faithfully
    D) Give Wisely
    E) Give without Seeking Recognition

    ANSWER) _____

Chapter 6
Tithing (10%)

"Is God really first in your life and you love Him, then you will worship Him and help spread His gospel? If you will show God that you love Him, He will bring so many blessing down from Heaven that you will not know where to put them all. But you must learn to put first thing first."

Let us examine life of a few people and see how they showed their love for God: In *Genesis 14*, we find Abraham giving something called a "tithe" to the priest Melchizedek after returning from the rescue of his nephew Lot from four enemy kings. When he encountered Melchizedek, he voluntarily surrendered to him one-tenth of all the spoils he had taken from his enemies. People sometimes argue that the tithe was part of the Mosaic Law and does not apply to modern-day Christians, who are not under the law. But Abraham tithed some 430 years before the Law was given to Moses. Furthermore, even in the days of Moses, the tithe was not a law although it appears in the legal book of Leviticus (*Leviticus 27*)

However, there is a consequence for not tithing: loss of blessings. From the above verses alone, it should be obvious that God owns everything, but just in case you are not sure, listed below are 3 more scripture references that state this very fact: ***Psalm 24:14, 1 Corinthians 4:7, and Deuteronomy 8:18***.

God told the Jews that He was the one giving them the power to make wealth. He owns everything, gives us the ability to make a living, and wants us to recognize that everything comes from Him.

We are simply stewards, or managers, of the things He has entrusted to us, and part of being a good steward is giving a portion of our earnings back to God. It's not that God needs our money. Rather, giving serves as an external, material testimony that God owns both the material and spiritual things of our lives.

How much is a tithe? - I believe that giving was meant to be individualized, even during the time of Moses. It was never intended that everyone should give the same but that each should give according to his or her abundance and conviction ***(1 Corinthians 16:2; 2 Corinthians 9:7)***.

One-tenth was the minimum standard, but the book of Deuteronomy lists several additional offerings described as tithes of a person's increase. Thus, it is likely that those who could gave much more than ten percent in those days.

Couples today who cannot commit a tenth of their resources to God should realistically examine their standard of living and spending habits.

Where should your tithe be given? - According to *Malachi 3:10*, the tithe was supposed to be brought into the storehouse, which was a place where the Jews delivered their offerings of grain or animals. The storehouse had specific functions, including feeding the tribe of Levi, feeding the Hebrew widows and orphans living within the Hebrew city, and feeding the Gentile poor living in the Hebrew city *(Numbers 18:24-29, Deuteronomy 14:28-29)*. Ideally, the local church could serve as the storehouse in God's economy today. God has designed the church to carry out vital social functions similar to those funded by the storehouse. Churches should also minister to the sick, teach families to care for themselves, and take the Gospel to the lost at home and abroad. Some churches do not minister fully in these areas.

Therefore, to the extent that a church lacks in a specific area of ministry, a portion of the tithe could be given to an individual or organization that is "filling in the gap." However, remember that you cannot sit under the teaching of a local church without supporting it financially. *(1Timothy 5:17-18)*.

Tithe from gross or net income? - There appears to be some confusion as to whether we should calculate our tithe based upon our gross income (before taxes and other deductions) or net income (after taxes and other deductions). According to the Word, God has asked for our Firstfruits, which is the first and best of all that we receive. Therefore, we should tithe from our gross, or total, income before taxes. When we calculate our tithes based on net income, we put the government ahead of God *(Proverbs 3:9-10)*.

Procedures for tithing – The word "tithes" is mentioned five times in Hebrews *(Hebrews 7:1-9)*. We bring our tithes and offerings; we present them to Jesus, our High Priest. Under the New Covenant and in this spiritual kingdom, He then takes those gifts before the Father. He ministers on behalf of the people, not on behalf of Himself.

When the people of Israel would go in before the High Priest, they were to verbally address him, meaning that time and care were taken. We should not just run in the church door and throw the offering in a basket.

It is necessary to present the tithes and offerings in a particular manner because of the abusive manner in which tithes and offerings were previously received. For examples of tithing applications.

Ten benefits (Rewards) of tithing:

I have also included Scripture references for you to check out.

1. **God is pleased with your obedience.** Regular giving is a sign of obedience to Christ. We prove our love for Christ by obeying his commands. (See Malachi 3:10; Isaiah 1:19)

2. **God is honor by your substance (money).** Proverbs 3:9 He deserves your faithfulness in giving your substance (money). (See Proverbs 3:9-10)

3. **Tithing helps to keep your priorities straight.** Matthew 6:21 I believe that giving to the Lord is the number one priority for a believer. (See Matthew 6:21)

4. **You are eligible for a blessing.** The blessing is not always monetary, but very could be a business opportunity, and invention, to write a book, and etc. God has blessed with a Covenant that promises "health and wealth" to the Christian that part of Salvation provision that must be claimed and beyond we as believers have an Inheritance. (See Malachi 3:10)

5. **Guards Christians from selfishness.** Tithing reminds us that ultimately our money does not belong to us. (See Acts 20:35)

6. **God loves a cheerful giver.** Are you excited about the opportunity to serve God with your finances? (See 2 Corinthians 9:6-12)

7. **Tithing supports the Great Commission.** Your tithe should go to your local church and God has chosen to work through the church during this age. (See Matthew 28:19,20)

8. **Tithing ensures that your needs will be met.** God has promised that our needs will be met. Needs – but not necessarily "wants". (See Matthew 6:33)

9. **Tithing helps to meet the needs of God's people.** Hopefully your church seeks to use at least a portion of its budget to help those less fortunate. (See 1 Corinthians 16:1,2)

10. **Tithing reminds us that God is the true owner and giver of all that we have.** All that we have belongs to God and the tithe helps to remind us of this fact. (1Timothy 6:17,18)

Please Note:

According to 1 Corinthians 4:7; (KJV) "For who maketh thee to differ from another? and what hast thou that thou didst not receive? now if thou didst receive it, why dost thou glory, as if thou hadst not received it?"

Chapter 6 Questions – "Tithing"

True or False

1. True ___ or False ___. Abraham gave Tithes before the Law (Genesis 14).
2. True ___ or False ___. There are many benefits to being a tither.
3. True ___ or False ___. There are penalties for not being a tither.
4. True ___ or False ___. The tithes are given to the house of God.
5. True ___ or False ___. There are procedures for presenting your tithes.

Fill in the blank

6. Based upon 1 Timothy 5:17-18, Who needs your financial support _____?
7. According to *Malachi 3:10*, the _____ is be brought into the storehouse.
8. Based Proverbs 3:9-10, Honor the Lord with _____ increase.
9. Based upon First Corinthians 4:7, what do you have that you did not receive _____.

Multiple Choice

10. What are some of the benefits (Rewards) of tither?

    A) God is pleased with your obedience
    B) God is honor by your faithfulness
    C) Tithing helps to keep your priorities straight
    D) You are eligible for a blessing
    E) Guards Christians from selfishness
    F) All the above

    ANSWER) _____

Chapter 7
Offerings

Tithe is an obligation, you give an offering freely, but you pay tithe. The tithe belongs to God. It is an obligation, and it is one you ought to want to do. You should love it when you find out the benefits of it. Tipping at a restaurant used to be 10 percent, and more than that in some places. God has never raised His percentage! It has been 10 percent for 6,000 years and look at the benefits you get for tipping God *(Psalm 91:16)*. You get divine healing, the Word of God, heaven, the Holy Spirit, Angels around you, protection everywhere you go.

Why wouldn't you want to give God a tip? Think about it: the richest being in the universe adopted you. Just think of it as tipping instead of tithing. Once you get into it, you cannot beat God giving. In the Holy Bible we have several types of offerings. In our research we are focusing on the monetary offering and that is essentially anything we give to God beyond the tithe. We should understand, therefore, that no giving can really qualify as an offering until the whole tithe has been given. For example, let's say you have heard that if you pay something extra each month on your mortgage you can pay your house off five years earlier. Imagine rushing into your mortgage company desiring to pay something extra and the customer service representative informs you that your mortgage payment for the previous month was never paid! How upsetting! On the other hand, imagine how delighted our Lord is, when we tithe and continue to give cheerfully above and beyond what he has prescribed.

The New Testament *(2 Corinthians 9:7, 8)* illustrates the type of giver that God requests us to be a "cheerfully". In the Old Testament, they not only lived off of the tithes but they also lived off of the offerings.

They did not only use the offerings for the building but for the upkeep of the Levites as well. The Old Testament also illustrates that there was a mixture. They did not quite divide tithes and offerings like some present-day Bible scholars teach: that tithe is tithe and offering is offering. Most importantly, they made sure they gave their tithes as well as brought their offerings *(Numbers 18:4)*. As found in the Old Testament, God not only gave the tithes to the Levites, He gave the offerings too.

We also find that terminology is so important. In the Old Testament, the word *offering* is a general word that is used to signify the coming forward and bringing of something unto God.

God wants us to see our money as something holy that we offer in worship to Him, and that without this offering our worship is incomplete. In *Exodus 23:14-15*, God gave regulations for every male among the children of Israel to come up to Jerusalem three times a year. They were to offer worship and to celebrate before God in the temple. Here is part of the regulation He gave:

> *"14Three times thou shalt keep a feast unto me in the year. 15Thou shalt keep the feast of unleavened bread: (thou shalt eat unleavened bread seven days, as I commanded thee, in the time appointed of the month Abib; for in it thou camest out from Egypt: and none shall appear before me empty"*

"No one is to appear before me empty-handed." This was part of God's ordinance for worship and celebration in the temple. Israel had to come up at God's appointed time and in God's appointed way, and no Israelite was to appear before Him empty-handed. Every Israelite had to have an offering for God as part of the celebration and worship. Whether it is a tithe, firstfruit or the actual offering, it is called the freewill offering. Please see (*Acts 2:42-47, Acts 4:32-37*) and (*2 Corinthians 8:9.*)

Offering is the bonus round of giving. It is our opportunity to find spontaneous or planned, sporadic or regular ways to exercise God's gift of a generous and thankful heart. For example, in the spirit of Firstfruits giving, one can make a tradition of setting aside any pay increase received in a month as an act of thankfulness for the increase in pay. (A great thing about this tradition is its painlessness.) But when the Spirit of giving really gets moving on people, watch out! Really great things are happening. A person or whole community of believers can be found sharing half or all their possessions or found giving even in poverty. Again, an offering is essentially anything that we give to God beyond the tithe.

Looking back on these topics of giving, we can now see that both tithes and offerings are indications and means by which God uses to finance the Gospel of the Kingdom. Giving is essential to the faith.

Chapter 7 Questions – Offerings

True or False

1. True ___ or False ___. Is the tithe an obligation that you must pay?
2. True ___ or False ___. Is an offering something that you give freely?
3. True ___ or False ___. Tithes and offerings are ways we can show God our true heart.
4. True ___ or False ___. As believers we are free to give our Offering as the Holy Spirit leads.
5. True ___ or False ___. Offering is the bonus round of giving, and providing believers an opportunity to receive additional blessings from God.

Fill in the blank

6. In the New Testament what type of givers does God request us to be (Second Corinthians 9:7, 8) _____?
7. According to *Malachi 3:10*, the _____ is brought into the storehouse.
8. What is a regular way to exercise God's gift of a generous and thankful heart _____?
9. Tithes and offerings are means by which God uses us to do what, _____.

Multiple Choice

10. In God's Financial Plan, Tithe and Offering are use:

    A) Type of giver that God requests us to be
    B) Part of the celebration and worship
    C) Tithing helps to keep our priorities straight
    D) Help us to not appear before God empty-handed
    E) Guards Christians from selfishness
    F) Returning to God what is owe to HIM
    G) All the above

    ANSWER) _____

Chapter 8
The Principle of Firstfruits

"Leviticus tells us that a tithe (not just a Firstfruits--as was mentioned in *Deuteronomy 14:23*) of the herd and flock also was holy to the Lord. An important distinction needs to be made here: the tithe and the Firstfruits are not the same thing." (*Pg. 4 www.houseontherock.net/spiritoftithing.htm*)

One of the most important laws of the Bible involves the principle of Firstfruits. It is the law of *first things first* and it has a fundamental impact on everything in your life. Understanding and living by this law helps you position yourself to receive the promise God has for you. **(Romans 11:16)**

"The first fruit offering always represented a future greater harvest. Whenever the Firstfruits offering was presented, you knew the harvest was coming." (*Pg. 1 http://www.emmanuelenid.org/sermons/Romans/Romans113.htm*)

Whatever you do with Firstfruits governs the rest and sets the pattern, or the promise, to come for the rest of whatever you establish. First things always belong to God **(Genesis 22:2, 1 Corinthians 15:23, and Romans 8:29)**.

Jesus was the firstborn and thus He was the Firstfruits. God wanted a family, He sowed a Son. That's why Jesus ascended from hell. See what He said to Mary Magdalene in **John 20:17**. He had to present Himself to God the Father as the Firstfruits. Mary understandably wanted to grasp Jesus tightly and keep Him with her. But He had to be the spotless Lamb and without blemish. He couldn't be tarnished. He became the Firstfruits offering so we might become sons of God.

This verse is saying every firstborn thing is devoted to God in a covenantal way. In other words, when you get your breakthrough, when you get that increase at your job, when anything new is established in your life, you must acknowledge the source of that increase. The first of that whole increase is devoted to God. The Firstfruits is not a tithe of the increase. It's the whole increase. What you must understand now is that all first things belong to God, even the first part of your day **(Psalm 5:3)**.

The first of everything belongs to God. He lays claim to it. Anytime something is called a "first thing," a "Firstfruits," or a "devoted thing," God always lays claim to it because He sees the Firstfruits as representing what comes after it.

The principle is that God sees all things according to how the first things are treated *(Romans 11:16, Exodus 22:29-30)*.

Jesus fulfilled the old covenant way of obeying this mandate. We do not sacrifice the firstlings of our sheep at the temple anymore or redeem our firstborn sons with gold. Jesus paid for all needed redemption. The principle established by the Exodus mandate remains. Today, we dedicate all our children to God, pleading the blessings of His new covenant over them. It may be appropriate, however, to make a special offering to the storehouse of God for your firstborn child just to acknowledge that all your children are a gift from God. God says first things belong to Him and He pursues covenant with first things to establish redeeming covenant with everything that comes after it. God said it is better to destroy a Firstfruits than to use it for your own personal gain. If you touch a holy thing, it will bring a curse on you and God says it is better to destroy that thing rather than let it bring a curse upon you.

TITHE VS. FIRST-FRUITS: I believe the body of Christ has been misled. You may have been taught that Firstfruits is your tithe. But your tithe is not your Firstfruits. Firstfruits is mentioned 32 times in the Bible. In Genesis 4, it is mentioned as "firstlings" or "Firstfruits." Tithe is also mentioned 32 times in the Bible but your tithe is first mentioned when Abram pays his tithe to Melchizedek *(Genesis 14:20)*.

The first-fruit is different from the tithe. The first tenth of God's daily provision (your regular paycheck or a bonus or any ordinary income or increase that comes as a regular part of God's provision for you) is the tithe. The Firstfruits is the whole of something given to you by God that represents all that comes after it. If the Firstfruits are sanctified to God—relinquished to Him in some way that worships Him—then all that comes after will be blessed. If the Firstfruits aren't sanctified to God, then they are judged as withheld from Him and the fruit that comes after will be cursed *(Proverbs 3:9-10)*.

Again, God says your tithe and your Firstfruits are not the same thing. The Firstfruits is the first of everything. After that, you tithe on everything else.

This principle is not limited to only your money. It includes your family, your time, your talent, and your gifts. It includes the first hours of your day, the first Sunday of every month, the first month of every year, the first of everything that sanctifies all that follows.

The point is to sacrifice something significant to you to exemplify to God that you are dedicating the very first of each year to Him, so that He will bless all that follows.

First things first; what you do first thing in the morning sets the rest of the day. You do not need to get up, get your coffee, and start doing your own thing. You need to say, "Good morning, Holy Spirit. I bless you today." You need to worship your Lord and hear from Him. Then, go get your day started and according to *Matthew 6:33*, all that you need shall be added to you.

Chapter 8 Questions – "The Principle of First-fruit"

True and False

1. True ___ or False ___. Jesus was the firstborn; therefore, He is the Firstfruits of God.

2. True ___ or False ___. First fruits always belong to God *(Genesis 22:2, 1 Corinthians 15:23, and Romans 8:29)*.

3. True ___ or False ___. God always lays claim on Frist-fruit because He sees the First-fruits as representing what comes after it.

4. True ___ or False ___. The law First-fruits and it's fundamental will impact everything in your life.

5. True ___ or False ___. First-fruits is what you do first thing in the morning that set up rest of your day.

Fill in the blank

6. The first _____ of God's daily provision or any ordinary income or increase that comes as a regular part of God's provision for you is the tithe.

7. The _____ is the whole of something given to you by God that represents all that comes after it.

8. You must understand that all first _____ belong to God, even the first part of your day *(Psalm 5:3)*.

9. According to Psalm 5:3, (NKJV). The Lord will hear my _____ in the morning.

Multiple Choice

10. The Firstfruits is the first of everything belongs to God:

    A) Your self
    B) Your money your family,
    C) Your time, first hours
    D) Your talent, your gifts.
    E) All the above

    ANSWER) _____

Chapter 9
The Principle of Sowing and Reaping

"The philosophy of the world is to get all you can, can all you get, and sit on the can. This isn't the way of the Kingdom of God." (Fitzgerald, (2005) Pg 1.)

Malachi 3, which we have read, gives us the background for God's financial plan. You see, there is no receiving without giving. That is just a divine law that works in every area of life, whether you are a Christian or not. The Bible calls it the Law of Sowing and Reaping. No matter what you sow, you will reap a result – and the reaping is always multiplied from what you sowed.

You can sow one corn seed and get a stalk with only one grain of corn on it. You get several ears a stalk with many grains.

There is multiplication in sowing and reaping. So, if you want to receive from God, you have to sow into the things of God. God has built into the system a channel to bless us so that we could become a blessing. The devil has tricked the church into believing that there is something intrinsically godly about deprivation and poverty.

He tells them that they will get theirs on the other side, so they really should not be concerned about getting any more in this life than just enough to barely make it. And while he is saying that, he (satan) and his cohorts are controlling the world and using up the resources that the Father put here for His people. Instead of children of God getting the benefit out of it, satan gets the benefits out of it. So that is the backdrop for all that we are talking about in terms of God's financial plan.

As mentioned before, *the way of the world is to get all you can, can all you get, and sit on the can.* **This is not the way of the Kingdom of God.** God operates His universe by laws that work when we apply the principles. They are as consistent as God Himself, Just as the Law of Gravity works every time, so does His laws concerning giving.

This is illustrated in *Luke 6:38*. Remember that we do not give to earn God's love. We give because we have already received His love, and from this place we operate in His principles. The Bible says that God gives seed to the sower. As we begin to prosper in His ways we cannot take credit, as He gave us the seed to begin with.

Mark 4 is a wonderful chapter to study, as Jesus teaches on this subject during the whole chapter. I encourage you to take time to study it. It teaches on different soils, sowing, and increase.

It is not wrong to expect a harvest when you sow. It is not selfish, unless our motives for wanting to receive are selfish. Every farmer expects a harvest from what he sows. Without a harvest, there is no seed to sow for the next harvest. But remember as your harvest arrives, don't eat all the seed, keep sowing. It is important not just to scatter seed anywhere but to find good soil and sow there. There is no return from sowing in bad soil.

God is always more interested in what we have than what we don't have. In *2 Kings 4: 1-7*, Elisha asks the widow, "What shall I do for you? Tell me, what do you have in the house?" The widow was telling Elisha what she did not have, but he wanted to know what she did have. What she did not have could not help her or anybody else. What she did have was the seed to her miracle.

The oil she had was small in amount, and she was asked to place it into large vessels. She could be excused for thinking that the little she had was insignificant. But sown in obedience to the prophet, it was multiplied and became a blessing to her and many others. Even in a time of need, taking a financial seed and sowing it in good soil is our way into the provision of God.

The Kingdom of Heaven is built on generosity and giving because the answer to the need is always in the seed. Never think your seed is too small to sow into a large ministry. Trees grow from mustard seeds and great oaks were once an acorn! Keep sowing!

Please Note as a Suggestion!
- **10% Tithing**
- **10% Sowing Seeds (Sow a seed to meet a need)**
- **10% Saving, learning to pay yourself**
- **70% Make the necessary adjustment to accomplish this**

Chapter 9 Questions – "The Principle of Sowing and Reaping"

True and False

1. True ___ or False ___. There is multiplication factor in sowing and reaping.

2. True ___ or False ___. Sowing and Reaping is a divine law that works in every area of your life.

3. True ___ or False ___. You get several ears of corn on a single stalk from one grain of corn.

4. True ___ or False ___. To receive from God, you have to sow into the things of God.

5. True ___ or False ___. Every farmer expects a harvest from what he sows.

Fill in the blank

6. No matter what you _____, you will reap a result – and the reaping is always is a multiplication of what you have sown.

7. God has built into the _____ a channel to bless us so that we could become a blessing.

8. It is important not to _____ seeds anywhere, but you must find good soil to sow.

9. The Kingdom of Heaven is built on generosity and giving because the answer to the need is always in the _____.

Multiple Choice

10. In *2 Kings 4: 1-7*, Elisha asks the widow, "What do you have in your house?

   A) Nothing
   B) She had some pots.
   C) She had some oil the seed that was key to her miracle.
   D) All the above

   ANSWER) _____

Chapter 10
Everybody Has A Seed!

Within the Word of God there is a principle of seedtime and harvest *(Genesis 8:22)*. If you really think about it, everything began with a seed. You and I as human beings all started out as a seed *(Genesis 1:9-12)*. So regardless of who you are, you have something and as a person of faith God can take whatever you have as a seed. I remember hearing the story of a particular young man in a particular service. When the offering was taken during the service and the plate was passed to him, the only thing that he had to give was a pencil.

God honored his act of faith and today he is a well- known minister of the gospel and has a TV broadcast that is seen around the world. If you do not have a seed, God has promised to give you a seed *(2 Corinthians 9:10)*. Most Christians never take time to study this principle. As I examine the above verse of scripture, I see it as win-win situation for me. Why? Because God has promised to give me the seed and all that He asks of me is that I plant it in the ground as He instructs. He will multiply the seed that He told me to sow, but that's not all; He will cause it to produce a harvest enough for me to have something to eat (minister bread for my food), and enough that I can plan again (increase the fruits of my righteousness). I do not know about you but I think that is a pretty good deal--all I have to do is obey Him.

We need to understand this principle of seedtime and harvest. *"...we must recognize 1) the purpose of the seed, 2) the process of the seed, 3) the power of the seed and finally, 4) the sowing and planting of the seed."* (Pg.7 You Have Something by Dr. Leroy Thompson Sr.)

In sharing with you God's plan for financing the gospel of the Kingdom of Heaven, this principle is very significant in the economic system of God. There must be a seedtime if you are going to have a harvest. Most people want a harvest time without a seedtime *(Acts 20:35)*. The world has a saying: "get all you can, and sit on all you get." In the economics system of Heaven, it is just the opposite *(Luke 6:38)*.

1. The Purpose of the Seed: The seed is to produce a harvest so that you can fulfill God's assignment, but most of us are in such a financial mess that we need help first.

When we give, our giving will produce receiving; our receiving will increase to the next level. *"Let me explain what I mean. For example, when being led by the Holy Spirit you give $100; that $100 is not leaving you.*

Using the principle of seedtime and harvest time, it just became your employee. It will begin to work for you as a servant to make money for you and bring it back to you." (Thompson, 2003, Pg. 18)

2. Your Seed is Powerful: God is revealing to us divine principle because He wants us blessed. Sometimes if we are not careful we underestimate the potential of a seed. An example of this can be found in *Genesis 26:1-5*.

3. The Power of the Seed: Never underestimate the potential of a seed. In *Genesis 26: 12*, Isaac received a hundredfold return. According to the Word of God, we never know what a seed can produce, but one thing I do know is that you cannot beat God by your giving *(Luke 6:38)*. There is no limit on what God can do. This is a spiritual law and it will produce supernatural results. Spiritual laws cause us to tap into another realm, another dimension *(2 Corinthians 9:10; Ecclesiastes 11:1-3)*.

4. The Process of the Seed: The word "sow" means to plant seed for growth by scattering or to scatter (as seed) upon the earth for growth.

First - thing you must remember is to always give God your best seed. To do that you must listen to the Holy Spirit and obey Him. Sometimes the best seed may put a strain on you, but that is okay.

Secondly - the sower's heart – that's yours-- must be in your sowing. For example, when offering time comes around, do not just pluck a few bills in the bucket with the rest of the congregation because it is the right thing to do. No! The sower must know what he or she is doing. Sowers have expectations of a harvest. Every time you plant, you make a demand on that seed and therefore you make a demand on the harvest, do not turn it loose, and do not let the devil send you a seed and you call it a harvest. When it is a harvest, you will not be able to carry the harvest in the same container in which you carried the seed.

Thirdly - understand the soil. As you are sowing to God the best seed, check out the soil. The seed and the soil never limit God. It is always satan or the sower who limits God.

Finally, *(Ecclesiastes 11:4)* will help you understand this principle. What is the meaning of 'he that observeth the wind'? *"It means if you are waiting for everything to get right before you start sowing – the economy, the stock market, your job, your boss giving you a raise – you will not sow. You must sow by faith, even though it looks like your company is about to shut down. If God told you to sow that seed, sow it, because He is trying to get you out of the financial mess you are in."* (Thompson, 2003, Pg.50)

The objective is that as you go through the process of sowing a seed and reaping a harvest:

1) You break free of the world system, which is most important.
2) You should become a tither on a regular basis.
3) You should be in a position where you will have more than enough to meet your needs and be able to help finance the gospel of the Kingdom of Heaven.

This was God's intent from the very beginning but we, His children, did not realize how caught up we are in the world's system. Thank God, He has provided a way for us to break free. Just keep on sowing! Please see **Appendix B.**

Chapter 10 Questions – Everybody Has a Seed!

True and False

1. True ___ or False ___. There is a divine law of seedtime and harvest.

2. True ___ or False ___. Everything began with a seed.

3. True ___ or False ___. There must be a seedtime if you are going to have a harvest time.

4. True ___ or False ___. Seeds are design to produce a harvest so that you can fulfill God's assignment.

5. True ___ or False ___. Your Seed is Powerful

Fill in the blank

6. The Process of the Seed: The word "sow" means _____ by scattering or to scatter (as seed) upon the earth for growth.

7. First, you must remember is to always give God your _____ seed.

8. Second, the sower's _____ that is yours must be in your sowing.

9. Third, you must understand is the _____ as you are sowing to God the best seed.

Multiple Choice

10. The objective of sowing a seed and reaping a harvest is to:

   A) Break free of the world system
   B) To position you where you will have more than enough
   C) To help finance the Kingdom of God on Earth.
   D) All the above

   ANSWER) _____

Chapter 11
Tracking Your Seed

"Let a man so account of us, as of the ministers of Christ, and stewards of the mysteries of God. 2 Moreover it is required in stewards, that a man be found faithful. 3 But with me it is a very small thing that I should be judged of you, or of man's judgment: yea, I judge not mine own self."   1 Corinthians 4:1-3;

Purpose

This chapter will aid you in understanding how to Track your seed from a spiritual perspective. Tracking is a feature that is available via the internet. The tracking feature gives details (date and time) of when a package will be delivered or received. You do not need the internet to track your seed as you do a package. In order to track your seed you need prayer and faith. In this chapter you will learn about praying the prayer of faith and the importance of sowing a seed. We must be obedient to God when sowing a seed and remember the Kingdom of God operates upon truth, honesty and integrity.

Recently I mailed a package at the local post office, and one of the options that were offered was tracking. When tracking a package via certified mail, log onto a computer, select the tracking option and confirm.

The tracking feature will give details of the exact date & time that a package will be delivered or an expected date of delivery. In other words, using a tracking feature allows you to know exactly when a package will be received. Briefly, in a couple paragraphs I will share two examples. Also, I will define several terms that will help us to understand tracking from a spiritual perspective.

Illustration Step 1 Sowed (planting), Step 2 Watering, and Step 3 Received.

At one point in my life I wanted a 'Bose CD Player and CD Exchanger. I prayed the prayer of FAITH and believed and that I received it.

A) On October 14, 2010 (DATE AND TIME OF RELEASING YOUR FAITH); My 'Bose CD Player and CD Exchanger' and I sowed a seed of $40.00 into Bill Winston Ministries.

B) On March 11, 2011, (DATES OF WATERING MY SEED SOWN) I sowed another seed of $25.00 into Antioch Christians Center for my 'Bose CD Player and CD Exchanger that I believed I receive.

C) On June 9, 2011(DATES OF WATERING MY SEED SOWN) I sowed another seed of $100.00 into 700 Club for my 'Bose CD Player and CD Exchanger' that I believe that I receive.

D) On August 9, 2011 I sowed another seed of $20.00 into Christ for all nation ministries for my "Bose CD Player and CD Exchanger" that I t believe that I receive.

E) On September 11, 2011, (DATES OF WATERING MY SEED SOWN) I sowed another seed of $100.00 into Pastor Naomi T. Hopkins of Refreshing Spring Christian Ministry, and I added a request for 3 CD's (Becoming, by Yolanda Adams, The Sound, by Mary & Mary, and Hello Fear, by Kirk Franklin.)

F) On October 27, 2011, (DATE HARVEST MANIFESTED) I received a check in the mail for $10,000.00 that cover the cost for the Bose CD Player and CD Exchanger ($749.00), the three CD's valued at ($45.00), plus the tithing from that harvest is always more than the amount of seeds sown ($415.00) and what you are believing God for.

Again, I want you to know that God is faithful to His word, and as a child of God all we have to do is take Him at His word and act on it. Please know that God is not limited to the mail box, He manifests the harvest however He chooses. The Word works if you work it.

1. **Naming Your Seed (Money)** - Money can be used for multiplying your need. We use money for bartering. Money represents our life, and it is valuable. When you sow it you are to name your seed based upon whatever your situation calls for and confess the Word of God and standing on it.

2. **Scriptures You Are Standing On When Releasing Your Faith** – When we truly understand and operate kingdom laws and principles, God is obligated to his Word. We must have scriptures in order to know what God has promised. We can only lay claim on those promises through the knowledge of the Word of God. Within the Holy Bible we have God promises; we claim them and apply them to our life

3. **Persons, Ministries, Or Organization (Ground) Seed Sown into** – A person, a ministry, or an organization must operate in truth, honesty and integrity.

The world system or the kingdom of darkness is a system that operates by deceptions, lies, and all types of corruptions. The Kingdom of God operates based upon truth, honesty and integrity. If a person, ministry, or an organization is not operating within these guidelines it would not be considered to be good ground. Remember if the Holy Spirit is leading you to sow, just be obedient, because it is not always possible for us to know.

I remember one time I was watching a particular ministry, and I was about to sow into this ministry, but the Holy Spirit said "no".

4. **PRAYER OF AGREEMENT** – if you are married the scriptures says that your prayers can be hindered if spouses are not in agreement. If your spouse is not a Christian than it would be impossible for him/her to be in agreement, but the two of you must be in agreement. Please see chapter ten on the prayer of agreement.

5. **PRAY OF FAITH -** This prayer is when you present to God a list of what you are asking God for and believing that you receive them. From this point forward, thank God; and believe you received what you asked for until the manifestation of what you believe.

6. **DATE AND TIME OF RELEASING YOUR FAITH** – Write down and keep a note of the date and time you sowed your seed. I have asked this question of many Christians, "when was the last time you prayed for something specific and you received it"? Most of them did not know. That is why I suggest that you write down the date and time of your request.

7. **DATES OF WATERING SEED SOWN** – Once the prayer of faith is prayed, and the seed is sown, and while you are waiting for the manifestation of what you believe that you received, each time it crosses your mind, you should give God thanks by saying.

   "Heavenly Father, I thank you that I believe that I receive", this is called watering your seed by giving thanks, praising, and worshipping God.

8. **DATE HARVEST (MANIFESTATION) WHAT YOU BELIEVED THAT YOU RECEIVE** – When the thing that you believe that you receive manifests, write the date and time and give praise and worship unto God that you now have it, and this ends this particular transaction with God.

Special Note: In tracking your seed, this mechanism is meant to be use as a tool that will help you be a good steward, managing what God has entrust you with, but it is never meant to put limits on God, nor an attempt to buy a blessing.

YOU CAN MANAGE YOUR SEED BY TRACKING.

1. **Naming your seed (money)** – You sow it and name your seed based upon your need and confess the word of God.
2. **Scriptures (God's promises)** – God is obligated to his word. We claim them and apply them to our life.
3. **Sow a seed (ground)** – Based upon truth, honesty, and integrity.
4. **Prayer of agreement** – (when appropriate).
5. **Prayer of faith** – You ask God, you believe that you will receive. Thank God.
6. **Date and time of releasing your faith** – Write down the date and time of sowing your seed.
7. **Dates of watering seed sown** – Once the prayer of faith of is prayed and you are waiting on the manifestation, continue to give thanks, praise, and worship God.
8. **Manifestation** - What you believed that you receive is in your possession!

Chapter 11 Questions – "Tracking Your Seed"

True and False

1. True ___ or False ___. Tracking your seed, is a means of stewardship.

2. True ___ or False ___. In order to receive a harvest you must sow into good ground.

3. True ___ or False ___. Is naming your Seed scriptural?

4. True ___ or False ___. Good ground can be a person, ministry, or an organization.

5. True ___ or False ___. The prayer of Faith is a necessary part of Sowing a Seed and receiving a harvest process.

Fill in the blank

6. The Process of Tracking your Seed, after the prayer of Faith is prayed you must record the _____, the _____ when your seed is sown.

7. Good ground is determine by the _____, _____, and _____ of the person, ministry, or an organization you are sowing into.

8. What must you do while waiting for the manifestation of what you believe that you receive as the seed has been sown? _____.

9. If married what can a Husband and Wife do to cause their prayers to be more powerful? _____.

Multiple Choice

10. What are the seven steps to "Tracking your Seed"?

    A) Naming your seed (money)
    B) Having scripture bases that promises what you are sowing for.
    C) Having good ground (person, ministry, or an organization).
    D) The Prayer of Agreement.
    E) The Prayer of Faith.
    F) Date and Time of releasing your Faith.
    G) Dates of Watering your Seed.
    H) All the above

    ANSWER) _____

Section IV

The devil diabolical plan is to bring humans into bondage through the influence of his demonic forces operating behind the scenes.

Chapter 12
The "Rat Pack" of Hell

The "Rat Pack" of Hell, satan's diabolical plan is to bring humans into bondage through the influence of his demonic forces operating behind the scenes. These demonic forces are listed below and I refer to them as the "Rat Pack" of Hell. There are other spirits that satan also uses to wreak havoc in our finances, but these are the main spirits that will be discussed in the following chapters.

1). the spirit of mammon
2). the spirit of greed
3). the spirit of poverty

These spirits work behind the scenes and cause five financial cancers in the earth today:

Premature death from living a fast life to make fast money!

- Debt
- Loss of assets
- Worry
- Heart attack and stroke due to financial stress

We must willing to learn about the origin of these deadly spirits, how to recognize when they are operating against you, and how to exercise your authority against them and prevent their infection of any of the five financial cancers in your life.

In *Matthew 6:24, Jesus says* "No one can serve two masters; for either he will hate the one and love the other, or he will be devoted to one and despise the other. You cannot serve God and wealth."

What is mammon? The word 'mammon' comes from an Aramaic word that refers to the inappropriate desire and pursuit of wealth. Mammon is not money. Many people do not understand this. Some versions of the Bible even translate this verse as "You cannot serve God and money." Now while that may be true, that is not what this verse is saying. There is nothing moral or immoral about money. It is completely amoral.

The spirit of mammon is the ambassador of satan who attempts to seduce us into putting money before God. In other words, mammon is not money - it is the dark spirit who seeks to seduce mankind through addiction to wealth. The world is held in the grip of the spirit of mammon.

The devil is driving and manipulating this world and its inhabitants by the incessant pursuit of financial gain. Since money and the possession of it is the way to attaining all the greatest and latest "creature comforts," mankind is driven by the desire for economic success like never before.

The priorities of nations, the politics of government, the policies of education and even the practices nowadays of religious activity are more and more being assessed and determined by economic considerations.

The primary motivation of mammon is fear; it is enveloped with a spirit of greed, it has a heart of deception and it does not provide what it promises. Instead it leads to bondage and to death.

satan tried to attack Jesus with a spirit of mammon when he offered him more wealth than anybody in this world has ever known. He said, "All these things will I give You, if You will fall down and worship me."

Here are some characteristics of people controlled by mammon:

1. Acacquiring money by takes precedence over obeying God
2. They struggle to give freely - normally giving reluctantly, out of duty and not love, never knowing how much is enough
3. They have a spirit of greed
4. They have a lack of contentment
5. They often have uncontrollable debt
6. They are victims of their own impulsive buying
7. They worship at mammon temples (we call them shopping malls) and they draw money from the offering machines (we call ATMs). If they do not have money, the priests of these mammon temples will always empower them to worship (we call that the credit); to buy things they do not want with money they do not have to impress people they do not like (we call that the icy stranglehold of deferred insolvency).

I call these malls "temples" because mammon competes for your worship, love, affection, loyalty and service. It tempts you to put personal gain before walking in the truth. That is why Jesus says that you cannot serve God and mammon.

The word 'cannot' does not mean that it is illegal but that it is impossible. It is not a matter of permission but possibility. You see, both God and mammon are competing for your worship and your service.

You can only (not may only, should only or even will only) serve one. So make up your mind one way or an other. Why? **Because you will outwardly serve what you inwardly treasure.** This can be seen throughout the Bible. Allow me to point you to a few quick examples:

    B) Gehazi - (2Kings 5:1-27) Gehazi had been a faithful servant to Elisha and served him with righteousness and integrity in everything. One day the spirits of mammon and greed got the better of Gehazi.

Naaman had just been miraculously cured of his leprosy by dipping in the river seven times and wanted to give Elisha gifts to say thank you, but Elisha, I believe, discerned a wrong spirit, so he turned it down.

Naaman leaves, but Gehazi runs after him and profits himself from the anointing that was on his master. When he arrives home Elisha asks him where he has been. He lies and says, 'Your servant went nowhere.' Elisha discerns the spirit of mammon, judges it and turns the leprosy of Naaman onto Gehazi - and we never hear of him again.

    C) Judas is another example. He sold out the Lord for thirty pieces of silver. That is the essence of the spirit of mammon - the same one that got all over Gehazi. The same thing happened to Ananias and Sapphira. What did it produce? death. That is the spirit of mammon.

Chapter 12a Questions – The Spirit of mammon

True and False

1. True ___ or False ___ mammon is money.

2. True ___ or False ___ mammon is a spirit?

3. True ___ or False ___ Do the spirit of mammon desire worship?

4. True ___ or False ___ Do the spirit of mammon have a temple?

5. True ___ or False ___ Is the spirit mammon competing with Almighty God for your money?

Fill in the blank

6. The spirit of mammon is what _____ for satan.

7. Where is the spirit of mammon temple? _____.

8. What gift of the Holy Spirit can be used to expose the spirit of mammon? _____?

10. What is the primary motive behind the spirit of mammon? _____.

Multiple Choice

10. What are some characteristics of the spirit of mammon?

   A) Acquiring money by takes precedency over obeying God
   B) Struggling to give freely
   C) Have uncontrollable debt
   D) Uncontrollable buying
   E) All the above

   ANSWER) _____

The Spirit of Greed,

Greed - *"You shall not covet your neighbor's house. You shall not covet your neighbor's wife, or his manservant or maidservant, his ox or donkey, or anything that belongs to your neighbor."* **Exodus 20:17** *"But I trust in you, O LORD; I say, 'You are my God."* **Psalm 31:14**

There are at least three forms of greed:
1. Obsessive desire for ever more material goods and the attendant power
2. Fearful need to store up surplus goods for a vaguely defined time of want
3. Desire for more earthly goods for their own sake.

Greed is the desire to have what someone else has and is really the basis for almost all forms of sin. Every war in history was fought because someone wanted to occupy a space on planet Earth that another group of people inhabited. Many marriages have been torn apart and children have suffered because one woman desired another woman's husband.

Greed for Power - In this form of greed, earthly goods are chiefly a means to an end, which is really not that far off from a healthy view. Money, real estate and cars are simply objects used to achieve, wield and display personal power. These objects can be used to intimidate or bribe others, reinforce one's own illusions about what is important or to build up a feeling of success. These are the "products of wealth," as the Jethro Tull song ("Slipstream") puts it.

The real problem here is more the desire for power than the actual greed. A common thread for sin in general is fear. A fear of helplessness or loss of control can turn into a lust for power as a way of preventing an undesirable situation. The parable of the man with an abundant harvest is well worth considering.

To destroy our desire for power, we must be generous in granting power to others. When appropriate, be submissive to others. Avoid jobs that are a temptation for a "power grab." Share credit for successes with others and claim your fair share of responsibility for failures being blamed on others. The idea is to stop trying to control everything and everyone. In parenting, this includes encouraging children to find their own way and respecting their choices.

It does not mean abdicating legitimate responsibilities, but loosening our grip on others' lives as well as our own. God will take care of us, He has the plan. We can't control everything anyway, so we might as well learn to relax in God's hands.

Greed is Born out of Fear - Fear is a poor motivator for virtue, but an excellent one for greed. Sometimes, greed is simply a desire to have so much that we cannot possibly run out. The stock market could crash, we could lose our jobs or health or we could be sued. If we acquire enough stock, real estate, or T-bills, we think we will be safe from want. This is an illusion. There is no perfect preventative for want, but even if there was, it would stand in opposition to the trust in God to which we are called. Jesus said, *"Perfect love casts out fear." (1 John 4:18)* Trust in God frees us from a need to build a massive buffer against poverty.

Part of the cure may be to embrace a certain level of poverty. We may not become homeless, but we can learn to do with less. Serious campers try to leave their campsite in the same state they found it. Ideally, there should be no trace left when they move on.

In the same way, try to use less of the world's goods. "Live simply, that others may simply live." Once this kind of freedom is practiced, we realize that we don't need that much, anyway. This knowledge, in turn, reduces our fear and builds a kind of strength and confidence.

The Greed of Acquisition - This is slavery, plain and simple. We can reduce ourselves to a small and cold desire to accumulate more electronic gear, trading cards, antiques or other collectibles. It is far beneath the dignity of human beings to enslave themselves to objects of their own making. It is well said that our possessions in some ways may come to own us. The obvious cure is to divest oneself of as much as possible, but another suggestion might be to consider the grave.

When we die, we take nothing with us. If we are bound by "disordered attachments" to worldly goods, the separation forced upon us by death will be even more painful. If we are destined for eternal glory, the temporary enjoyment of trinkets in this life is simply absurd. Meditation on this begins to loosen the grip of objects on the heart.

Many people have been shot to death because someone desired to have something that they were without — and for some reason or another — felt that they deserved it. And think of the multitudes of criminals who break into houses, steal cars and other possessions belonging to other people every few seconds across the United States.

All of these sins have one thing in common — Greed!

Unfortunately, human beings are born with this trait in them; but as we grow up and become more intelligent, we have to find ways to subdue this part of our character. Some ways to do this are listed below:

1. Think about the short time span you are on this Earth. Is the greed you have for something belonging to someone else really worth the moment of pleasure that you will derive from it should you get it?

2. If you have the desire to steal whatever it is that will make you happy, consider the fact that you must hide the truth (tell a lie) for the rest of your life so you are not caught in your actions. In other words, if you rob a grocery store and get $50, is that act worth hiding for the rest of your life? You will have to keep it on your mind constantly in order to avoid people finding out about the robbery, your getting caught and sent to jail. Is $50 really worth all this hassle? If so, you really do not value yourself very highly.

Greed does not start out on a large scale. A normal person does not just wake up one morning and decide to rob a bank. Instead, sin starts out small. A person becomes angry at themselves for not having more money, a better job, more friends or a prettier face and body than someone else. They begin to feel sorry for themselves and instead of doing something about it they look for ways to wallow in their self-pity. They find themselves saying things like, "She always has money and I work harder than she does.

Life is meant to be enjoyed. In fact, it takes more time and trouble to plan, conceive and carry out revengeful acts of greed (that usually blow-up in your face) than it does to simply be peaceful and keep your mind clear and pure.

If you always tell the truth, you do not have to worry about telling different lies and trying to remember "who" you told what lie to. It gets boring going through life looking over your shoulder all the time.

Mankind always wants more than what they have. Where does it end? If you get the million dollars, will you be satisfied and stop there? No, you then want another million. Only God can help you recognize greed when it starts and help you to defuse it.

Again, we must learn to depend on the leading and gifting of the Holy Spirit. The gift Ddiscernment of Spirit will us to recognize a wrong spirit, so he turned it down.

Chapter 12b Questions – "The Spirit of Greed"

True and False

1. True ___ or False ___. The spirit of greed is obsessive with desire.
2. True ___ or False ___. Greed is born out of fear of not having enough.
3. True ___ or False ___. Greed does not start out on a large scale.
4. True ___ or False ___. The spirit of the greed requires Acquisition.
5. True ___ or False ___. The spirit of greed will you to steal when there is really no need?

Fill in the blank

6. When under the control of the spirit of greed. Once you get your first million, what will you want to do? _____.
7. Is the greed you have for something that belonging to someone else really worth the _____ you have commit to get it?
8. What gift of the Holy Spirit can be used to expose the spirit of Greed? _____?
9. What is the primary motivation of the spirit of Greed? _____.

Multiple Choice

10. What are some characteristics of the spirit of Greed?

    A) Disobey God when it comes to handling money.
    B) Giving out of duty
    C) They often have uncontrolled debt problems
    E) Victim of Impulsive buying
    F) All the above

    ANSWER) _____

The Spirit of Poverty

God, our loving Father has revealed His will for his children. *(John 10:10)* There is a false doctrine that believers should be poor and suffer from financial insufficiency.

This is a false doctrine is to keep you from enjoying the blessing of God. The purpose of poverty is cause you to reject what God has offer. as the Holy Bible is concerned, Christians are not supposed to be in poverty of any kind evidenced by several scriptures in the Bible: *3 John 1:2; Psalm 84:11; Psalm 37:25; 2 Corinthians 8:9; Deuteronomy 8:18,* just to name a few.

The spirit of poverty gives people the wrong mindset, that they should not a lot of money

The Holy Bible says we should prosper in every area of our lives: Spiritually – *(John 3:16, 17)*; physically – *(1 Peter 2:24)*; mentally – *(1 Timothy 1:7)*. We must understand that there is an underlying cause for financial challenges in the church and in our individual Christian lives. There is a battle for your finances; it is a spiritual battle and we have some financial straight talk about it. Jesus said *"The Spirit of the Lord is upon me because he has anointed me to preach good news to the poor. He has sent me to proclaim freedom for the prisoners and recovery of sight for the blind, to release the oppressed, to proclaim the year of the Lord's favor."* (*Luke 4:18, 19*.)

My understanding, based upon this scripture, is that we should not be poor any more. The Bible did not say that people should run after money and forget God. Many members in the body of Christ mistakenly think that poverty is just the absence of money. That is not totally true even though money is needed to meet your basic daily requirements for a good life. If you are unable to meet your financial and other essentials needs that make for a good living, the spirit of poverty is in place *(Proverbs 24:4, Luke 16)*.

We must recognize that the spirit of mammon operates along with the spirit of poverty. He collects the money and is responsible for sending forth the spirit of poverty that is attacking the human race. This spirit of mammon seems to be giving a lot of people money, but only after he has afflicted them with the spirit of poverty.

He then gives them money so that they will be blinded and go to hell fire. One of the examples that often comes to mind is what we see happening in the rap world.

It seems as if they, *"the rappers they seem to come out of nowhere and stardom "stars" overnight and very shortly after stardom they have been killed in shootouts." (Pg 1, it's always the good ones that have to die by www.epinions.com).*

I am just using rappers, but the same scenario happens in many other areas also. Following are some examples showing just when a spirit of poverty is at work:

The Sign of the spirit of poverty is at work

"When somebody has sufficient income and is still having problems financially- inability to keep a job, inability to eat normal food others eat, etc.; always being duped or regularly attacked by thieves; being surrounded by poverty stricken relatives. The spirit of gambling is another example of poverty: "The devil tells you to play again and you will win, and you end up losing. You may even keep playing until you have lost all your possessions. When you have health problems that require a lot of money is another form of poverty as well." (Pg 3 Olukoya, 2005) www.montain-of-fire.com/spirit_of_poverty.htm.

Retaliations against the spirit of poverty

When all these things are happening to you, then you must learn the art of aggressive praying. Often, instead of praying, you blame others for what is happening *(Ecclesiastes 6:1-2)*.

The Bible says a lot about being poor, but Christ has redeemed us from the curse of the law. Salvation is freely offered to us. All we have to do is receive it by faith; but getting the message of salvation to people, along with teaching them about the victorious lifestyle in Christ, costs a lot of money. We must realize that God want us blessed in every area of our lives, and that includes financial prosperity.

Christians easily understand that it costs money to buy gasoline to operate their cars, pay taxes and put roofs over their heads, and they have no problem understanding that clothing their body costs money.

When it comes to the Gospel, somehow they have this weird idea that the money will just fall out of the sky from heaven. Victory comes through surrender - it is not ours, it is His. **(Psalms 50:7, 9-12)**.

"When we grasp this revelation, the next step is surrender. We must surrender ownership of our possessions, surrender the illusion that we are in control and surrender our will to the reality that... it's all His. Surrender first involves repentances for past financial sins. Scripture repentance refers simply to a changing of direction from our way to God's way.

Once we have repented, we can then begin the process of renewing our minds through God's word to become better stewards over all that He has temporarily entrusted to us.

So what is the point? Why the constant financial struggles? Why all theses Bible verses about money?" (Pg 8, Money Came by the House the Other Day by Robert Kotz).

The point is beyond what many of us might ever imagine. God uses our finances to develop our character. Jesus uses parables regarding financial stewardship to teach us about the importance of developing Godly qualities such as perseverance, discipline, charity, compassion, sacrifice, integrity and honesty.

Money is an ideal training tool because God knows where your treasure is. **(Matthew 6:21)**.

The goal of stewardship is much greater than simply paying your monthly bills. The goal is preparation for eternity. The eternal stakes are so high that it becomes our duty to learn all that we can about stewardship, which brings us to the next fundamental truth; No one was born with financial wisdom (Hosea 4:6).... and few are taught it. Yet, every day we are faced with countless financial decisions that we are unprepared to deal with.

"We can't steward what we don't understand and this lack of knowledge creates a spiritual vacuum. A spiritual vacuum will never remain empty – one of two things will happen. It will be filled by a proper relationship with the Lord, or satan will continually entice us to fill it with counterfeits." (Pg 10 Money Came by the House the Other Day by Robert Kotz.)

"For example, the devil uses the world system to try and deceive us with the lie of the self-made man. Many falsely believe that we are in control and that the answer is found in more money, more lifestyle and more power. The message ingrained in us from childhood is to seek success, not a Savior, and satan whispers to us, You don't need the Lord, you need a Lexus." (Pg 10, Money Came by the House the Other Day by Robert Kotz)

Jesus knew the truth. That is why over half of the parables in the Bible deal with economic matters. Do not be confused by fact that He spoke in terms of grapes and wine, bread and oil, sheep and cattle... that was the medium of exchange, the money of His day.

He spoke in terms very real to the people of that time and His message then, as now, is very simple...seek wisdom. Then we will be transformed into wise stewards. Please refer to (**Proverbs 1:7, Deuteronomy 8:18, Proverbs 3:1, 13-17**).

As we recognize what has taken place because of the fall of humankind, we must know that as Christians, as citizens of the Kingdom of Heaven, God as provided a way that we can overcome all the tactics of the enemy. Regardless who you are, God has blessed you with something. I remind you of the story I mentioned earlier.

Several years ago, I heard a story of Christians in a particular service. When the offering plate was passed around a particular person gave the only thing that he had - a pencil - and God honored it. Today he is known around the world as a man of faith. We all can see from this example that everybody has something.

Chapter 12c Questions – Spirit of Poverty

True and False

1. True ___ or False ___. Poverty is a spirit, that cause you to have wrong mindset?

2. True ___ or False ___. The spirit of poverty has a purpose?

3. True ___ or False ___. Can you tell when poverty is at work in our lives?

4. True ___ or False ___. The spirit of poverty has signs that it is working in a person life.

5. True ___ or False ___. Poverty is mindset that is implanted in mind of its victims?

Fill in the blank

6. What is the purpose of the spirit of poverty? _____.

7. Once you recognize the spirit of poverty is at work in your life, what must you do. _____.

8. The Bible says a lot about being poor, but Christ has redeemed us from the curse of the law. What does this mean to you as a believer? _____.

9. We are not born with financial wisdom. What must we do what to get wisdom? According Proverbs 23:23; (KJV) _____.

Multiple Choice

10. What are some characteristics of the spirit of poverty?

    A) Always broke
    B) Do not feel they should have money or material things
    C) Have a mindset of unworthiness
    D) Spend money unwisely
    E) Impulsive buying when you get money
    F) All the above

    ANSWER) _____

Section V

The choice is yours, Switching from the kingdom of darkness to the Kingdom of God! God has provided a way for us to break free of the world system, and fulfill our destiny.

Chapter 13
Switching Systems – switching from kingdom of darkness to the Kingdom of God of doing things

In the previous chapters we have shared what we believe to be the problem that is causing the financial challenges of the church. As I mentioned before, the church is not the building but consists of believers of the Lord Jesus Christ who have been born again.

In this chapter we want to explain how to switch from operating in the kingdom of darkness (the world's system) to operating in the Kingdom of God (the Heavenly system). We have been physically born into the world and we have been educated by the world's system, so it is only natural that we follow the world's way of doing things. Now that we are born-again and have been translated into the Kingdom of God, we must switch our mode of operation to that of the heavenly system. For example, I have seen a cartoon of a young boy who saw a cookie in the cookie jar and he simply had to have it. While no one was watching, he stuck his hand in the cookie jar to grab the cookie.

When he tried to take his hand out of the jar, he found that he could not hold onto the cookie and take his hand out because the opening was too small. He could hear his mother approaching but would not let go of the cookie and got caught. The reason he got caught was because he refused to let go. Many Christians are in this same predicament. They have received the Lord Jesus Christ as their Lord and Saviour and are now citizens of the Kingdom of Heaven but they continue to hold onto the world system or operating in the way of the and are continually "caught" or trapped by the enemy. We, who are familiar with the world system, know that it is corrupted and is coming to an abrupt end.

We also know that satan is the god of the world system (**2 Corinthians 4:3, 4**). As born-again Christians, and as citizens of the Kingdom of Heaven, we must come to the realization that *"the earth is the Lord's and the fullness thereof"* (**Psalm 24:1**), and that God has created everything for His sons and daughters and it belongs to us through the blessings of Abraham. Although the devil (or heathen) is now occupying it and has control of it, we must learn the ways of the kingdom of Heaven and follow them, thus separating the devil and his heathen (or his human representative) from our rightful possessions (**Colossians 2:15**).

The devil will be unable to stop us from processing what is rightfully ours if we operate in the ways of the Kingdom of Heaven. For instance, what we say and how we speak is very pivotal to operating at a higher level. If we continue to follow the world's way of doing things, saying what we have always said, doing what we have always done, we will continue to fall into the trap that has been set by the enemy. It is important to change what you do and say to agree with what the Word of God says. The Bible says, *"to whom you yield yourself* [I'll add, your words and actions] *their servant you become"* (**Romans 6:16**).

As citizens of the Kingdom of Heaven we must learn the operation of the Kingdom of Heaven and put it into practice in our everyday lives; it's not something that we do only on Sunday. There is no reason for the church to be as broke as it is when we have been given Kingdom of Heaven principles by which we are to operate! There are three primary subsystems that satan uses to deceive and enslave humankind; the religious system, the political system, and the economic system. Our focus will be on the economic system.

In **Genesis 12:1**, we see how God extracted Abraham from the worldly economic system by faith. In order to understand this better, we must examine the system of the world compared to God's system that operates by faith. In the Bible there is a system that is defined as the <u>mystery of Babylon</u> **(Rev 17:5)**. The Babylon system is a demonic system and its primary objective is to influence people to work and gain prosperity independent of Almighty God. The purpose of the Babylon system is to have its participants rely on their own ability—so people are actually being deceived and seeing themselves as acting independently of any system.

The result is that those who operate "on their own ability" (the Babylon system) are falling into the trap of the enemy whose primary desire is to enslave you and ultimately capture you for eternity. Although the world's system sounds simple, it is designed for you to work for a living, but never sets you free from the cycle of using your ability to make money any way you can. God's system, on the other hand, is designed to free you from bondage while believing and receiving by faith.

Operating in faith in the Lord Jesus becomes a lifestyle that surpasses the subject of money; it becomes a lifestyle of believing and receiving by faith that is as simple as breathing.

Steps to Move from the World's System to God's System

Listed below are steps designed to assist you in moving from the world's system to God's system. Some of these steps have been previously discussed. As you prepare to switch systems, it is helpful to follow these steps in chronological order. As you practice them, you will receive that which the Word of God has promised:

Step One - You must be a person of <u>FAITH</u>

In order to be a participant in the things of God, you must be **<u>BORN-AGAIN</u>** (*John 3:3 and Romans 10:9, 10*), and one is born-again by receiving Jesus as your Lord and Saviour. When you become born-again, you are translated from the kingdom of darkness into the Kingdom of God, and you become a citizen of the Kingdom of Heaven (*Colossians 1:9-14*). This places you in a position to become a partaker of the inheritance that God has for us.

Receiving the Lord Jesus Christ as your Saviour and Lord is only the beginning and everything that we do in the Kingdom of God must be by faith. Simply put, faith is nothing more than acting on what you believe; and in our case we believe that the Holy Bible is the Word of God from Genesis to Revelation. As the Holy Spirit reveals the promises of God, we act on that WORD and receive by FAITH what God promises, whether it is salvation, healing, provision, or whatever as long as it is in line with the Word of God.

Step Two - You must walk in <u>LOVE</u>.

Based upon *Romans 5:5*, the love of God is shed abroad in your heart by the Holy Spirit when you become born-again. With the love of God being in our hearts, we have the ability to walk in love as our Lord requires based upon the commands that we have been given in *Matthew 22:37, 38*; *John 13:34* and *1 Corinthians 13:4-8 AMP*.

Step Three – You must be <u>A PERSON OF INTEGRITY</u>

The world system or the kingdom of darkness is a system that operates by deceptions, lies, and all types of corruptions. The Kingdom of God operates based upon truth, honesty and integrity.

If you are to have the promises of God manifested in your life, you must live what is called a clean life, and what the Bible calls a holy life.

This does not mean that you are perfect, but you strive for righteousness such as admitting when you have made a mistake, walking in unselfish behavior, having the right motives for operating in the Kingdom of God.

Step Four – You must be a **TITHER.**

As shared in Chapter 3, tithing has been designed by God as a means to keep within the covenant that He established 400 years prior to the giving of the law (*Genesis 14:20*). Tithing was practiced during law (*Leviticus 27:31*) and as citizens of the Kingdom of Heaven, we continue to practice even the dispensation of grace (*Hebrews 7:5-9*). Tithing also shows that we are in partnership with God helping to carry out His will and His work.

Step Five – You must be a **SOWER**

I remember a conversation that I had with a particular person and we were discussing different types of games. He made the statement that you got to put in to win, and this is true with the law of sowing and reaping; you must sow if you want to reap. Note: God has designed for us to receive through our giving; this is the reason that we give. You do not give simply to get because God is the one who blesses us with the seed.

Please read *Proverbs 11:24-25* from three different translations, so that we can fully understand what God is saying regarding our giving.

> **Proverbs 11:24, 25 (KJV)** *"There is that scattereth, and yet increaseth; and there is that withholdeth more than is meet, but it tendeth to poverty".* 25 *"The liberal soul shall be made fat: and he that watereth shall be watered also himself."*
> **Proverbs 11:24, 25 (Amplified)** *"There are those who [generously] scatter abroad, and yet increase more; there are those who withhold more than is fitting or what is justly due, but it results only in want."* 25 *"The liberal person shall be enriched, and he who waters shall himself be watered."*
> **Proverbs 11:24, 25 (New Living Translation)** *"It is possible to give freely and become more wealthy, but those who are stingy will lose everything."* 25 *"The generous prosper and are satisfied; and those who refresh others, will themselves be refreshed."*

God does not respond to need; God is not moved by your need. God does respond to faith; God is moved by faith. You can need all you want, you can pray all you want, and you can cry all you want but applying your faith to Gods' Word and sowing a seed will cause Him to act on your behalf.

Just look at what is happening around the world; you can see that this is true. The Bible is the Holy Word of God, and it depicts how God thinks and how God acts (*Isaiah 55:8-11*).

There is a shortage mentality in the world today. We say there is a gas shortage, water shortage and so forth. In the Kingdom of God there is no shortage, and as a citizen of the Kingdom of God you do not have to live on the same worldly level as people who do not know God.

In *1 Kings17: 8 – 16*), we have the story of the widow to whom God sent His prophet, Elijah. We briefly discussed this story in the chapter on the principle of sowing and reaping, but we are now about to take a closer look. If you examine these verses of scripture carefully, you will see how God thinks and acts. Of all the people to whom God could have sent His prophet, He sent His prophet to this widow. Notice the instruction of the Lord to the widow from the man of God (again God is not moved by your needs). Notice that the woman did according to the instruction of the prophet Elijah (to fix him a meal first, and bring it to him so he could eat).

To help you understand what is happening here, the widow was to fix the prophet a meal first, then bring it to Him. She and her son were to watch the prophet eat, and then the widow was to go and fix a meal for herself and her son. Now think about it for a moment; you can imagine the thoughts that the devil might have tried to put into her mind, but still she obeyed in faith. If you notice, God sent Elijah the Prophet to the widow when she had only enough meal for herself and her son. In essence, through His instruction, God was leading her to sow because she needed to release her faith so that He could be released to move in her situation.

Again, God is not moved by need. The God we serve is a God of love, but as you and I can see many are the needs around the world, but God is not moved by them for this reason. He has bound Himself by His Word, and He cannot violate His Word for ANYONE; no matter how long you cry, no matter how long you fast.

The reason that the law of sowing and reaping cannot work without your applying it is simple: it is not a promise, but a law and the only way this law will work is by applying this principle. If you do not believe this, put it to the test.

You will see that nothing will happen through prayer alone, but if you give in faith and pray, stand back and watch this law produce for you.

This is a hard word for some people to understand but it does not change. You can examine your Bible and you will find example after example. Again, God is not moved by needs, but He is moved by sowing seeds in faith. Understand that when this principle is applied, God will move in your situation.

This teaching is being brought forth because God has a plan; His only plan is to meet the needs of His people through the law of sowing and reaping and we cannot change that. God needs your seed because He will not violate the covenant that He made with the earth *(Galatians 6:7 and 2 Corinthians 9:5-10)*.

The Spiritual Law of Sowing and Reaping

The **SEED** must first be sown: You must sow a seed in order to reap a harvest. God promised that He will supply the **SEED**. The **SEED** must be sown into good ground *(Matthew 13:3-9)*. You must sow in proportion to your need or the obligation that you desire to pay off *(2 Corinthians 9:6-10)*.

<u>Please review the following examples of obligations:</u>
1. **To be bless with something!** that you want for enjoyment from a Christian Perspective Say for instance various books and DVDs of various Christian programs valued at $300. Seek God for the seed amount and the soil to sow and when you sow your seed, be sure you give it an assignment.
2. **To bless someone with a $1,000.00** – seek God for the seed amount and the soil to sow and when you sow your seed, be sure you give it an assignment.
3. **Sears Card** – Balance of $3,000.00 – seek God for the seed amount and the soil to sow and when you sow your seed, be sure you give it an assignment.
4. **Master Card** – Balance of $4,500.00 – seek God for the seed amount and the soil to sow and when you sow your seed, be sure you give it an assignment.

5. **Students Loans** - $10,000.00 – seek God for the seed amount and the soil to sow and when you sow your seed, be sure you give it an assignment.

6. **Car #1** – Balance of $13,000.00 – seek God for the seed amount and the soil to sow and when you sow your seed, be sure you give it an assignment.

7. **Visa Card** – Balance of $15, 000.00 – seek God for the seed amount and the soil to sow and when you sow your seed, be sure you give it an assignment.

8. **Car #2** – Balance of $25,000.00 – seek God for the seed amount and the soil to sow and when you sow your seed, be sure you give it an assignment.

9. **Home mortgage** – Balance of $175,000.00 – seek God for the seed amount and the soil to sow and when you sow your seed, be sure you give it an assignment.

10. **Dream Home mortgage** – Balance 0f $1,000,000.00 – seek God for the seed amount and the soil to sow and when you sow your seed, be sure you give it an assignment.

The above list provides examples of obligations that might have been accumulated by an individual. This individual can pay off these obligations by applying the principle of the Kingdom of Heaven (sowing and reaping).

A Tither you can move into the principle of sowing and reaping and as you begin this process, seek your Heavenly Father for the seed amount that is needed to meet each obligation.

Once you get the revelation from the Holy Spirit, the next step is to find out the specific ground that the **SEED** is to be sown in (remember you must give your **SEED** an assignment). You must sow your **SEED** in faith (mix faith with your seed) and then you must wait for harvest time.

Now understand this: applying this principle is not a hard thing, it is just hard on the flesh. Why? Because something on the inside of us has been programmed to not let it go, in God those that withhold will come to want, and those that scatter will increase. When you study and mediate on this, it will convert your thinking.

If you will renew your mind to operate in this principle, you will find yourself beginning to sow left and right; but if you just sit there, God will let you sit there. Remember God said fear not, because the law works by faith.

Step Six – **NEVER DOUBT**

Once you sow do not let doubt come in, because doubt will stop the supernatural from working. Please do not associate with the nay sayer, because the content of their conversation will cause you to doubt.

If you operate in this principle with all seriousness and without doubt, you can stop every need. All you have to do is renew your mind in this area, listen to the Holy Spirit and sow with an expectancy.

Remember you are giving to receive (there must be an expectancy). God has already given to you so you have the seed, now you have to give to receive.

Let me reiterate that God's plan is to meet your need through giving. Your job is not your source; it is only one resource that God uses to get the seed to you, but if you are not careful, you will make your job your source as have many Christians. God is your source. *(John 3:16; John 12:23-24);*

Summary – We have to renew our minds in this area so our flesh will not fight us on this principle. There is no way that you can operate in lack again if you know how to apply this law of sowing and reaping. You can put an immediate stop to every need through this principle. When you understand this law, you will recognize that was put in place back in the Garden of Eden and it is still is for us today. It is time for us to break free of the world's system operating in this principle in our everyday lives.

Example: How you can put this principle into practice:

Let us say you are born-again, you are working, you are walking love, and you are a tither. You have a desire to go on vacation in Hawaii, and this vacation would cost $5,000. The world's way of paying for this type of vacation is to save for it or put it on a credit card. Now as a Christian, you are not to do things according to the world's way, so you have to shift to a higher level in order to break free of the world system. As you move to this higher level of operation, go to your

Heavenly Father and ask Him for the seed that you need in order to go on this vacation.

The seed for $5,000 is $500, but it is up to God how a seed will produce. Ask your Heavenly Father, He will cause the $500 seed and He will cause it to come into manifestation. There is no way to say how the $500 will come to you. It might come as a bonus from your job; it might come as gift from a total stranger. Now when the $500 manifests, ask God where He wants you to sow; no matter who it is or what the person is doing, just be obedient to God (follow His simple instruction no matter how strange it might seem to you from the natural perspective). Sow in faith believing that you are doing what God has instructed you to, and do it with an expectation (your expectation is the harvest of $5,000). As you are waiting for the manifestation, continue to give God praise.

In my personal experience, you will normally have a manifestation in about thirty to sixty days depending upon the faith of the person. Operating this way puts you on a whole different level. The $5,000 comes in you go on your vacation and have a great time, and when you return you do not owe anybody anything. This will work for whatever need you might have. Through this process you can be debt free, and not owe anything to the world. The vacation is just an example; you can apply the same steps to pay off existing bills or make desired purchases. The objective is to remove yourself from the debt which causes you to be controlled or bound by the world system. One last thing: when you plant the seed, know that the harvest will always be more than enough to meet obligations. If the harvest is not enough to meet a particular need then the amount that you received is probably a seed. You must plant it and continue the process until the harvest is more than enough to meet the obligation that you are believing God for.

Chapter 13 - Questions - Switching Systems

True and False

1. True ___ or False ___. There two kingdoms on planet earth?

2. True ___ or False ___. The kingdom of God is truth, honesty and integrity.

3. True ___ or False ___. The kingdom darkness operates by hook or crook (John 8:44)?

4. True ___ or False ___. Christians lives should be governed by the law of Seedtime and Harvest.

5. True ___ or False ___. To understand the Kingdom of God's operation you must renew your mind based upon Romans 12:1-2

Fill in the blank

6. When you operate the law of Seedtime and Harvest, you are you identifying with the kingdom _____.

7. What is the method of operation of the Kingdom of Heaven based upon Colossian 2:12? _____.

8. What are the five steps to switching systems? _____, _____, _____, _____, and _____.

9. Operating in faith in the Lord Jesus must one become a _____.

Multiple Choice

10. The five steps that a Christians must put into practice in order to rise above the world system?

    A) You must be a person of FAITH
    B) You must walk in LOVE.
    C) You must be A PERSON OF INTEGRITY
    D) You must be a TITHER.
    E) You must be a SOWER.
    F) All the above

    ANSWER) _____

Chapter 14
Investing in the Kingdom of God

"The purpose of life is not to live a low risk-high comfort life. The purpose of life is to know God intimately and then to partner with him in building his kingdom. Now I find that thrilling. God wants me to be his business partner. How cool is that? And just like the master does in this story, God gives us some stuff to do that with. He gives us time, some talent, and some money. Then He says, what I want you to do is invest some of this – just like a business partner would – invest some of this kingdom business." *(2005, Pg 1 "Investing In The Kingdom", 2005, http://www.fpcbellevue.org/sermons/)*

What talents and resources has God blessed you with? Has God shown you how to employ what He's given you for his kingdom? What are some of the excuses we might use for not serving God with our talents and resources? How does our use of what we have been given reflect who our true master is? In raising these questions, there are scripture verses I would like for you to examine - *Matthew 25:14-30*.

This is a fearful passage to read, but it's an important one for anyone claiming to be a Christian. Like the master in the parable, God gives us talents that he expects us to invest for his kingdom profitably. Every day we have opportunities to use and multiply these talents for God. If we are faithful and obediently invest, God will be pleased with us and increase our responsibility in His kingdom. If we do not obey, knowing God's will for us to invest, we risk being stripped of what he has entrusted to us and invite his discipline.

"For instance: if, as your IRA, you put $1,000 in a hole in the ground for one year and inflation is 3% that year, your $1, 000 will only buy $970 worth of groceries when you dig it back up. And, if you had to pay 25% federal income tax on that money (in addition to the inflation loss) your $1,000 would actually buy only $727.50 worth of groceries! So, by burying your $1, 000 in the ground, it would be worth less than $730 in one year! And, of course, state and local tax would only make the value lower! (2005, Pg. 2 "Investing in the Kingdom", http://www.fpcbellevue.org/sermons/)

We can start the investment process now by taking stock of the talents God has given us. He has uniquely given every person resources for use in his kingdom on earth.

Since God has given us the resources, we know He expects us to invest them wisely. Once we've identified them, we can then ask God to reveal the time and opportunities to invest daily.

A few examples are evangelism, intercessory prayer, financial giving, exhortation, helping widows or the poor, and exercising special gifts in ministry (music, teaching, administration, exhortation, healing, prophecy, etc.).

"Well, in this parable, two of the three servants followed through on a plan to double their master's money. How many of you know the rule of 72? It tells you what you have to do to double an investment. Let say you have $5, 000 and you want to double it to $10,000 in 10 years. You take 72, divide it by 10, and you get 7.2. Right? This means you have to get 7.2% return on your investment in order to double your money in 10 years. If you want to turn that $5,000 into 10,000 in 7.2 years, you would divide 72 by 7.2 and get 10. You'd find that you need to get 10% per year return on your investment in order to double your investment in 7.2 years." (2005, Pg 2 "Investing in the Kingdom", //www.fpcbellevue.org/sermons/)

It is no wonder that the master in this parable was angry with the servant who kept his money...who buried it in the ground. What a waste! How irresponsible! We will experience great joy as our investments are multiplied in God's kingdom. God will bless us with more and reward us when he sees that we have been faithful.

How to Continue Your Legacy

I have a suggestion on how you can continue your legacy. When you purchase a life Insurance policy for covering your final expenses. Why not add an additional $10,000 or more and leave it to your home church to help continue the spreading of the Gospel of the Kingdom of God.

Chapter 14 Questions – Investing in the Kingdom

True and False

1. True ___ or False ___. God has blessed you with skills and abilities.
2. True ___ or False ___. God has blessed you with certain talents.
3. True ___ or False ___. God has blessed you with gifts.
4. True ___ or False ___. God expect a return on His investment (Matthew 25:14-38)?
5. True ___ or False ___. Are you using your talents, skills, abilities, and gift for Almighty God's glory?

Fill in the blank

6. What talents do you have _____?
7. What skills do you have _____?
8. What abilities do you have _____?
9. What gifts do you have _____?

Multiple Choice

10. In the parable of the talents (Matthew 25:14-38). Why was the giver of the talents angry with the servant who buried his talent in the ground? When God give you something, it is an investment in you, and He expects a return.

    A) He was wicked
    B) He was slothful (lazy)
    C) He was unprofitable
    D) He was unbeneficial
    E) None of the above
    F) All of the above

    ANSWER) _____

Chapter 15
The True Reason for Prosperity

We have covered many aspects of how to obtain your financial freedom but there one more thing I need to share with you: the reason for prosperity. I trust by now you believe that it is the will of God that we prosperity in every area of life. We have defined four different aspects of prosperity:

- **Spiritual prosperity** - being born-again – *John 3:16*
- **Soulish prosperity** - being made whole and at peace in your mind and emotions – *Romans 12:2*
- **Physical prosperity** - being made whole in your physical body and walking in divine health – *Isaiah 53:5,6*
- **Social prosperity** - one who has status in the community
- **Financial prosperity** – being a position that we are not only can me your need but meet someone else needs – *Mal 3:8-12; 3 John 2;*

There are people who claim to have a problem with prosperity, but notice how many of them go to work every day to pay their bills and live a comfortable life. Is this not seeking prosperity? Perhaps they have a different view of the meaning of prosperity. What if a question regarding prosperity were posed to the American public at large? My question would be:

What is the reason for prosperity? - "I would dare to say that most people say because I want a better house, I want a better car and etc. I would say from observation that as soon as a person gets a promotion or a significant salary increase they go out and buy a bigger house. More expense car, and before they realize it, they are right back in the same predicament that they were in before they got that promotion or significant salary increase. (2003, P.1. Price, the True Reason for Prosperity)

"I have another question? When is the house going to be big enough? When are the vehicles going to be big enough? Why do you want a big screen TV in every room? If you are not careful this is what most people in general think is the reason for prosperity." (2003, P.1. Price, the True Reason for Prosperity)

Let me say this: our loving Heavenly Father has no problem with us having these things. As a matter of fact that is one reason that they have been created, they were created for us as His children to enjoy.

We need to be careful, if we think that is the only reason we are to prosper. Allow me to share with you a little Biblical history. Please refer to *Genesis, Chapters 17 – 25*.

God raised up a man by the name of Abraham and blessed him. The Bible said that Abraham was very rich, and through him, God raised up a nation by the name of Israel. This nation was one of the wealthiest nations on the face of the earth; they were also one of the most feared. Their God was the most feared of all gods upon the face of the earth. The primary reason that God bestowed such favor upon the nation of Israel was to glorify Himself; so that the rest of the world could see the awesome God that Israel served to provoke a holy jealousy in the people of other nations to the point that they would approach the nation of Israel and ask them about their God.

This would give Israel a chance to testify about the goodness of their God, thus causing the other nations to be proselytized, and become worshippers of the God Israel. If you examine the first five books of the Bible, you will find that the nation of Israel decides to keep the goodness of God to themselves.

A great many of Christians today are spending their wealth on themselves, or should I say they are keeping it to themselves. The reason for prosperity is specifically stated in the book of **Deuteronomy** (*Deut. 8:17, 18*).

Our God is a good God, and as He has blessed you with what you currently have, ask yourself this question: are you using your blessing for His glory or your own. If you are, then it is likely that you will not receive more. Remember, the primary reason for prosperity is to establish God's covenant.

God says He gives us the power to get wealth so that He may establish His covenant, not our agendas. Paul said in a section of the New Covenant, "we are laborers together with God." In another place, he says we are workers together with God, not for God.

The Lord does not need us to do anything for Him. He is very capable of doing everything for Himself. He does give us the privilege to do something with Him. There is a big difference in doing something for someone and doing it with someone.

Another very important point this verse makes is that it takes wealth to establish God's covenant, and that He has put the power to accumulate that wealth in the hands of His people (**Luke 19:9-10**).

Historically speaking, the Lord is talking (***Deuteronomy 8:18***) to Israel, but He is also communicating with all His children in the Body of Christ, even in our own time. Notice, He says, '... you shall remember....' That means He does not want us to forget. Jesus does not say He came to work miracles, although He worked miracles.

He did not say He came to raise the dead, even though He raised the dead. He did not say He came to feed the multitudes with a few fish and loaves or to quiet the raging seas but He did all those things. Actually, all of the miracles and all of the signs that Jesus did were done to advertise His seeking and saving that which was lost.

Think about it: He did not raise everyone who was dead. He did not heal everyone who was blind or sick. He did not cast out all the devils and demons in the earth-realm. He did enough to advertise His presence. His true purpose was, and still is, to seek and to save the lost. That is the heart of God. That is His covenant, and that is what we, the Body of Christ, need the wealth for (***Matthew 6:33 KJV***).

"This verse and the two passages that precede it comprise the foundation for the purpose of prosperity. Most Christians seek first their own well-being but Jesus instructs us to seek first the kingdom. He does not say to seek only the kingdom; He says seek first the kingdom. If you do first things first, then everything else will fall into line as it should. But if you do not have everything in the proper sequence, you will end up struggling and struggling, as many believers are doing today." (2003, P.1. Price, The True Reason for Prosperity)

Chapter 15 Questions – True Reason for Prosperity

True and False

1. True ___ or False ___. Spiritual prosperity is the most important of them all. (John 3:16)

2. True ___ or False ___. Physical prosperity is being made complete in your physical body and walking in divine health. (Isaiah 53:4-6)

3. True ___ or False ___. Soulish prosperity means being made whole and at peace in your mind and emotions. (*Romans 12:2*)

4. True ___ or False ___. Social prosperity is being the go to person in the community.

5. True ___ or False ___. Financial prosperity – being in a blessed so that you bless be a blessing to someone else (*3 John 2*)

Fill in the blank

6. What are the five types of prosperity: _____, _____, _____, _____, _____?

7. What is the primary reason for prosperity? _____.

8. What are some of the other reasons for prosperity? To _____, and _____ the lost.

9. Paul said in a section of the New Covenant, "we are _____ together with God." In another place, he says we are _____ with God, not for God.

Multiple Choice

10. What is the true reason for prosperity?

    A) Our God is a good God
    B) To establish His covenant
    C) For His glory, to show what He can do.
    D) To seek and save the lost.
    E) All of the above

    ANSWER) _____

Appendix A
Keys to the Kingdom of Heaven

These appendixes are created to give you a more comprehensive examination of the concept of "keys" to operating in the Kingdom of Heaven. It is my hope that you now have a better understanding of how to use specific keys (laws and principles by which heaven operates) to open the doors that lead to financial freedom and that you will ultimately experience all that God has for you as you apply His Word in every area of your life.

Success in the kingdom of God is learning the keys (laws and principles by which Heaven operates).

When Jesus said that He has given us the keys to the Kingdom of Heaven He was not talking about physical keys, but about the principles and laws by which heaven operates *(Matthew 18:13-19)*. This manual was written to provide insight and understanding of these principles and laws so that you can apply your faith properly and experience financial freedom God's way. Once you take hold of these laws and principles, believing them to the point of practical application, you can face with confidence any situation with which you are confronted.

You must also learn how to apply the right key to the right situation. Just as a vehicle operates using only the key that is specifically designed for it, the same is true with the Kingdom of Heaven. This manual has outlined the foundational keys necessary to unlock the doors that lead to financial freedom such as giving of tithes and offerings, sowing seeds, applying your faith to God's Word, enacting the law of sowing and reaping, etc. You are now armed with the right keys that specifically apply to Godly prosperity. You would not apply through prayer scriptures concerning physical healing to experience an increase in your finances. To do this would be using the wrong key for your situation.

Keys are set up by God to produce a specific result that cannot be changed or altered. Your opinion, misguided prayer or your desire for a different outcome will not influence the result of a principle or law that has been set in motion by the Almighty God.

If you have what you feel is an unanswered prayer, examine the Word of God to see if you are trying to open some doors in heaven with the wrong key. Once you find the right key that applies to your situation and act upon it in faith, you will see God move in answer to your prayer and your situation will change.

To help you further understand that the result of enacting a law or principle is fixed, God gave us natural laws as well as spiritual laws. For example, there is the Law of Gravity. It is designed to pull everything to the center of the earth. Gravity is a law, it is a principle, and it is a key. This is how God set it up and man can do nothing to change it. You cannot defy gravity.

For example, if you climb to the top of a ten story building and jump off, gravity will have its way, pulling you down to the ground with the end result being your probable death. Another natural law is the Law of Lift. It is designed to supersede the law of gravity when the correct parameters are in place. A bird in flight is a perfect example. Birds were designed by God to naturally operate in the law of lift as their method of travel; we call this flying. Airplane travel is also an example of the law of lift in motion.

Some spiritual laws have been explained already in this manual such as the Law of Sowing and Reaping. This is a supernatural law that is activated through your giving. Though natural comprehension of this law eludes us as humans, we know that if we operate in it by faith, it will produce for us. With spiritual laws we may not understand how God does what He does, but He causes it to work for us. The key to successful life in the kingdom is learning its laws and principles. We may not fully understand how these laws and principles work, but our objective is to obey them.

There are six main points to focus on when implementing the keys that God has given us to obtain financial freedom:

    Access – the ability, right, or permission to approach, enter, speak with, or use; admittance, We have access to God Himself and all He owns when we operate in the Kingdom of Heaven *(Romans 9:4 NLT)*. For example, if I give you the key to my car, you now have access to my car and everything that is in it. It has been made available to you through the use of the key.

Authority – a power or right delegated or given As His children, God has delegated His power to us *(Luke 10:19 NKJV)* and given us the right through Him to call forth from the spirit realm into the natural realm whatever we need *(Romans 4:17)*. We must operate in the Kingdom Of Heaven to exercise our authority. Using the same example, when someone gives you the keys to their car, they have given you authority or the legal right to drive their car.

Ownership – legal right of possession we, as God's children, are joint heirs with Christ *(Romans 8:17)*. In the spirit realm, we already own all He desires to bless us with but we must operate according to His kingdom principles if we are to experience the natural manifestation of that ownership. For example, when you purchase a home or car and all the requirements have been met and all the papers have been signed, ownership transfers to you.

Knowledge and understanding applied – Your knowledge and understanding of the laws and principles of the Kingdom of Heaven must be applied in order to produce the desired benefit. Without application, the benefits are available but never actually realized or experienced. The Bible tells us that faith without works is dead *(James 2:20)*.

Power – (Authority) to permit or to prevent As His children, we can walk in our God-given power through prayer *(James 5:16; Matt 18:19)*. When we pray according to His Word and in faith, it releases God to move on our situation. Through the power of prayer, we can thwart or even stop the attacks of the enemy against our finances or any other area of our lives. God gave us His power over all the power of satan, our enemy *(Luke 9:1 Contemporary English Version)*.

Freedom – the right to enjoy all the privileges or special rights of citizenship, membership, etc. *(Gal 5:1 NIV)* When we become citizens of heaven, we are able to experience the peace and security of being in Christ *(John 14:27)*. We are able to cast our cares upon the Lord, being released from the pressure and stress of financial matters. To truly experience this kind of peace, we must operate in the freedom of the Kingdom of Heaven.

What is the purpose of a principle?
    1) Principles were created to simplify life for you.
    2) Principles were created to help protect and preserve your life.
    3) Principles were created to assist you in making decisions.

If you learn the principles of the kingdom, you will not have to pray for answers from God that He has already given as principles - principles designed to guide you in your decisions. Sometimes in our natural minds, we have a long list of do's and don'ts we think necessary to see God move after the expected period of interminable waiting. We tend to make life harder than He intended. His principles are designed to truly make life decisions a little easier for us.

Though Jesus had difficult periods in His life, His following the Father's principles helped Him to make simple decisions and to be at peace with them. He knew how to operate the keys, principles, precepts, and laws designed by His Father. **(Matthew 8:5-12)**.

Appendix B
Testimony of What a $500 Seed Can Do!

As you go through the process of sowing a seed and reaping a harvest, you should have the following objectives:

1. To break free of the world system;
2. To tithe on a regular basis;
3. To place yourself in a position where you will have more than enough to meet your needs and are able to help finance the gospel of the Kingdom of Heaven;

In September of 1999, I was working on a particular job and I came to the conclusion that it was time for a change. I was entertaining the idea of looking for another job, but I was not exactly sure what I wanted to do. I received a call a couple of weeks later from a recruiter asking if I was interested in changing jobs. I told him that I was entertaining the thought, but that I had not really reached a final decision. As the conversation progressed, the recruiter asked me how much I wanted to make per hour. I told him that I was willing to settle for $35 - $40 dollars per hour and he said, "Let's see what I can do." Around this same time I was preparing to visit my son at Norfolk State University and I had planned to visit a church in the area. I knew there was a week-long meeting going on at the church, and they were bringing in various guest speakers. I was familiar with their ministry. So I told my wife that since I would be in the area visiting our son,

I would stop in and visit this church. Over the course of the next couple of days as I was preparing for my short trip, The Holy Spirit spoke to my heart and said "I want you to sow a $500 seed in this particular ministry." I had become familiar with this principle and I shared with my wife what the Holy Spirit had laid on my heart. She was in agreement. As planned, I left on my short trip. I visited the church in the area and really enjoyed the meeting; the Holy Spirit really moved in the service. The Word of God came forth and I sowed my $500 seed as the Holy Spirit had instructed. I was truly blessed by attending the service and I returned home.

It was probably within a couple of weeks after sowing that I received a call back from the recruiter asking me if I was willing to go for an interview. I went on the interview and within two weeks I was offered a job with a starting salary of $75,000 per year, rounded out to be about $35.75 per hour.

In October of 1999, I started my new position. I believe that my being obedient to the Holy Spirit in sowing that seed is what caused me to be blessed with that new position. If you think about it, that was a great return on an investment of a $500 seed, but that is not all! That one seed is still producing today because over the last seven years I have had the privilege of making over $500,000; all because of a $500 seed. Some people have a problem with the hundredfold return, but what I know through experience is that there is an unlimited return on operating this principle.

Jesus said He gave us the keys to the kingdom, and as I mentioned earlier, these keys will cause "supernatural results" because we serve a supernatural God. As we take time to study what Jesus meant and apply His Word, we can experience the abundant life that Jesus came to give us, but we have to do it God's way.

How many chickens would you have to sell to generate $500,000? I remember a pastor sharing one time that the ladies in his church had labored all night one Friday night preparing chicken for dinners they would sell on that following Saturday. Well, the following Saturday came and by the end of the day they had only made $300 from their labor. They did not operate in the kingdom principles of the Word. The Word of God works if you work it. This was God's intent from the very beginning but because we have been ignorant of His instructions in His Word regarding financial matters, we got caught up in the world's system. Thank God He has provided a way that we can break free! Just keep on sowing!

Appendix C
Example of a Small Church with 250 Members Who Tithe!

God has a financial plan and it is simple and easy; all we have to do is our part. I am basing this example on a minimum of $25 per week and that is extremely low. In the state of Virginia, according to the U.S. Census Bureau, the average salary is $40,534 per year which averages at approximately $779.50 per week. All God asks for is 10% ($77.95) to help finance the gospel of the Kingdom of Heaven. In return He will bless the 90% that you have left.

If you had 250 member tithing $25 per week, the church income would be $6,250 per week.
1. If you had 250 member tithing $25 per week, the church income would be $25,000 per month.
2. If you had 250 member tithing $25 per week, the church income would be $300,000 per year.
3. If you start a second service and had 250 members tithing a minimum of $25.00 per week, the church income would be $600,000 ($300,000 x 2) per year.
4. If you start a third service and had 250 members tithing a minimum of $25.00 per week, the church income would be $900,000 ($300,000 x 3) per year.

I was a member of a church that put this very example into action and they were able to purchase eighty acres of land, build a new church for fourteen million dollars and paid it off in five years.

This church had 2,000 members and they had 4 services per Sunday. Do the math and you can see how easy this can be done.

2,000 x 25.00 = $50,000 per Sunday

I knew of another church that took up a special offering asking for $1.00 per member. Their collection totaled $2,000.00 per week for a special project.

See how the Word of God works! Unfortunately the devil has duped the world and a significant number of Christians along with unbelievers are in debt up to their eyeballs and are not in a position to tithe as little as $25.00.

Appendix D
A Successful Strategy for Raising Large Gifts for Small Ministries

In the State of Virginia according to U.S. Census Bureau, the average family income in most areas, are $25,000-$45,000 per year. The average family typifies this classification of potential donor. This group is the bread and butter future for your organization. They are the people who will give you time and talent in addition to money. There will be a few future big donors in this group. If their loyalties are garnered for your organization at this time, it will pay rich rewards over the next 20 years. These families can commit $25-$50 a month to your organization for a three to five year period and provide the solid financial base you need for growth. In addition, each of these families knows 10 to 15 other families who are in similar circumstances who would also listen to your story.

The volume of donors available from this income range of Christian families is unbelievably large. It is not customary for most church ministries to seek these families for large gifts. Most organizations head for the town's list of the 40 best known Christian business and professional leaders. These people were overworked long ago. I want to encourage you to go to a layer of the Christian community that is rarely talked to face to face for giving to any cause other than their church.

Appendix E
How to Open a Checking Account: Step - by - Step Guide

Please know that banks are not your friend, although they provide very friendly customer services. Banks are in business to make money by known, and unknown fees. Make sure you read all documents (the fine print), and choose your bank carefully. Personally, I prefer Credit Unions.

1. How to Open a Checking Account: Step-by-Step Guide
Reference https://wallethub.com/edu/how-to-open-a-checking-account/10299/#step-by-step

Opening a checking account — also called a "share draft" account at credit unions — is easier than you might expect. Perhaps the hardest part of the process is determining which type of checking account is suitable for your needs, and we already have you covered there with our quick reference guide and online comparison tool. You can complete your account application online or, if you would prefer, you can visit a local branch of the bank or credit union you have chosen.

In this guide, you will learn the steps of opening a checking account, what the general requirements are and how to select the right type of account and financial institution.

2. Before You Apply

In order to ensure you are applying for the right checking account, you are going to need to put in a bit of work before you actually start filling out an application form.

- A. **Identify Your Needs:** The right checking account corresponds to your individual needs and usage habits. So, before applying, ask yourself the following questions:

  - Do you want a checking account primarily to deposit your earnings, pay bills electronically, write checks, transfer money, make everyday purchases, or all of the above?

  - Will you need access to a physical bank branch or ATM network near your home, work, or school? On the other hand, could you get by doing most of your banking online and over the phone?

Do you want to have access to your own banks' branches and ATMs when traveling?

- How much money do you plan to keep in your account?
- Which matters more: an accessible bank or minimal fees?
- How important is it that your account balance earn interest?
- Do you qualify for any special accounts, such as those designed for students, seniors, or members of the military?

B. **Compare Financial Institutions and the Types of Checking Accounts They Offer:** Check out and find the best account for your own banking needs. Each financial institution's website will also have details on the checking accounts they offer.

As you review your options, do not overlook credit unions and online banks. Credit unions are member-owned non-profits that serve people who share an affiliation (e.g., those who work for certain employers or residents of a city or neighborhood). Online institutions, such as Ally Bank and Discover Bank, have few if any brick-and-mortar branches, so you may not have the option of banking in person. In return, you will generally get lower feels and higher interest yields on interest-bearing accounts.

Here is a quick list of some of the fees and features you may want to compare across accounts to find the financial institution that offers the most relevant services for you at the lowest cost:

Costs

Monthly service charges or maintenance fees
Overdraft or nonsufficient funds fees
Debit/ATM card fees
Low minimum balance fees
Online banking fees
Printed checks fees
Balance inquiry fees

Features
Limits on the number of transactions
Wait time for deposits to be credited
Check-writing privileges
Electronic banking options such as bill pay
Overdraft protection

Requirements
Minimum opening deposit
Minimum balance
Direct deposit

Determine Who Will Have Access to the Account: If you share personal finances with someone, you might also consider opening a joint checking account that you both can access. In your application, you would simply choose the option for joint checking (if available) and provide information for each co-owner.

Most banks and credit unions give you a choice between setting up an account online or visiting a nearby branch to open your account the old-fashioned way. Whichever you choose, opening an account follows the same general steps:

A. **Gather Your Application Materials:** Before you can complete an application, you will need the following three things:

- **Identification:** When opening an account in person, most banks require two forms of identification such as a Social Security card, driver's license, state ID, passport or birth certificate. If you are not a U.S. citizen, you may be able to open an account with identification issued from your home country. To apply online, you will need to supply your Social Security number, date of birth and the number of a government-issued ID like a driver's license. If you are applying for a joint account, both accountholders will need to provide identification.

- **Proof of Address:** To open an account in person, bring a lease or utility bill with your name and current address.

- **Opening Deposit:** Typically, a minimum opening deposit for a basic checking account is between $25 and $100, although it may higher for interest-bearing accounts. If you open your account online, you can pay with a credit card, debit card or an electronic transfer from a savings or checking account at another institution.

A. **Complete an Application:** Simply go to the application page on the institution's website or visit a branch location. Afterward, the institution will review your information. Typically, the bank will run a special credit check that provides information on your past banking history to determine whether to approve your account. If approved, you should receive documents that bear your new account number and routing number as well as other important account information.

B. **Sign a Signature Card/Account Documents:** This is the card to which, your signature will be matched every time you write or deposit a check. With many online-only institutions, you will be able to sign your paperwork electronically but some may require you to visit a physical branch to sign the signature card or to mail or fax documents.

C. **Make Your Opening Deposit:** Depending on how you make this payment, there may be a hold of a few days before your funds are available for writing checks, making withdrawals or making debit card purchases.

D. **Receive Your Account Tools:** Once your application is finalized, your deposit is made and your account set up by the bank or credit union, you will receive in the mail a set of personalized checks, deposit slips and, in most case, either a debit card or an ATM card. You will need to activate your debit/ATM card and set up online account access.

E. **Set up Direct Deposit:** Arranging to have payroll or government check directly deposited to your account is often required to avoid monthly fees or to get other benefits.

If you have chosen an account that requires direct deposit or simply want to take advantage of this convenience, you will need to talk to the payroll department at your employer, for example, to get the direct deposits started.

3. **Become familiar with Check Routing Number: What It Is & How to Find It.**
   Reference https://wallethub.com/edu/routing-number/14293/

   At one point, you may have been asked by a biller or your employer to provide your bank's routing number — usually in combination with your bank account number. And if you're part of a shrinking group of consumers who still issue paper checks, then you've probably encountered this mysterious code on your checkbook or deposit slip.

   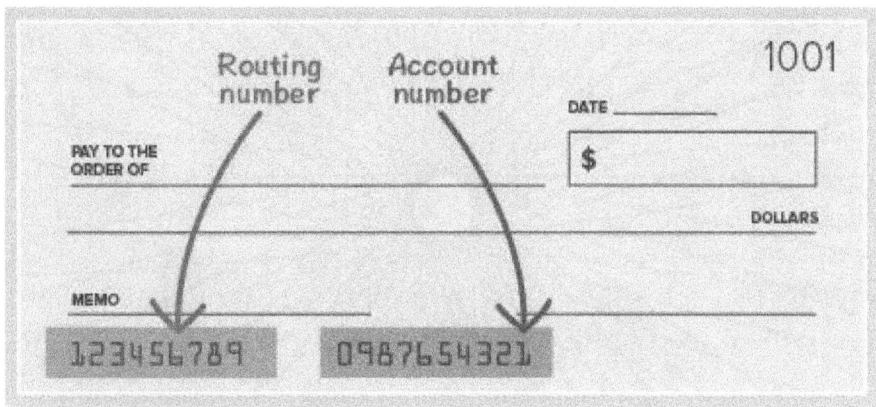

   The nine-digit routing number — also called the ABA RTN, or "American Bankers Association Routing Transit Number" — serves as an electronic address for bank transactions made among financial institutions within the U.S. (international transactions require different codes such as the SWIFT or IBAN).

   The ABA implemented this system in 1911 to automate paper <u>check processing</u>, and for decades, routing numbers have been printed on checks in a machine-readable format with magnetic ink. As electronic transactions grow more common, the use of routing numbers has expanded to accommodate <u>ACH and wire transfers</u>, as well as newer types of accounts such as prepaid cards.

   Below, we identify all the ways to locate the code and explain the steps you should take if your bank changes its routing number, which commonly happens after a bank merger or acquisition.

4. **Here are some things to be mindful of:**

    - **Follow Your Bank's Instructions**: Your financial institution will notify you of any routing number change months in advance. In many cases, the old routing number will be kept active for months or years after the new one is applied to your account. You will need to follow the instructions provided by your bank, but in many cases, they will permit you to keep using your old checks (with old routing numbers printed on them) until they run out. If they ask you to stop using your old checks by a certain date, it is OK to ask that they provide you with a free box of new checks.

    - **Reconfigure Automatic Transactions:** Even if you are given a lot of time to change over, it is a good idea not to delay reconfiguring automatic deposits and withdrawals with your new account information. If you continue to use an old routing number that your bank has phased out, your bank most likely will not honor a transaction bearing that code.

    - **Review Bank Statements:** To ensure that you convert over everything, it is a good idea to review your bank statements from the past 12 months. List all recurring automatic transactions, including direct deposits and automatic payments scheduled in (or outside of) online bill pay. For direct deposits, you may need to complete new paperwork and provide a voided check that reflects the new code. Having this list will ease the updating process and ensure that no payment or deposit is rejected by your bank.

Endnotes

Holy Bible (1997). Containing the Old and Test Testament Authorized King James Version Red-Letter Edition. Illinois: Tyndale House Publications.

(Retrieved 2008, Sept. 5, P.1.)
(www.kingdomfinanceseminar.com/welcomeminister.ph)
(Fitzgerald, (2005) Pg 1.) (Pg. 4 www.houseontherock.net/spirit_of_tithing.htm)

(Retrieved 2008, August. 5, P.1.)
http://www.emmanuelenid.org/sermons/Romans/Romans113.htm)

Investing In the Kingdom – (2005) P.1. "Investing In The Kingdom", 2005,
http://www.fpcbellevue.org/sermons/)

Epinions.com – (April 25, 2005 it's always the good ones that have to die)

Katz, R. W. (2004) Money Came by the House the Other Day) Florida: D C Press

Olukoya, D K (2005) P.1. www.montain-of-fire.com/spirit_of_poverty.htm)

Price, F. K. C. (1999) The True Reason for Prosperity. CA: Faith One Publishing

Thompson, L. (2003) You're not broke you have a seed. Louisiana: Ever Increasing Word Ministries Publishing.

Hayes, N. (1986,) Oklahoma: Harrison, Inc. (Retrieved November 25, 2008)

Dictionary.com - (November 25, 2008 www.dictionary.com)

(Retrieved March 10, 2006)
www.thegoodsteward.com/article.php3?articleID=970)

(Retrieved February 10, 2018)
How to Open a Checking Account: Step - by - Step Guide
https://wallethub.com/edu/how-to-open-a-checking-account/10299/#step-by-step

(Retrieved February 10, 2018)
Become familiar with Check Routing Number: What It Is & How to Find It.
https://wallethub.com/edu/routing-number/14293/

Decision Page

To receive Jesus Christ as your own personal Lord and Savior

The Bible says in *1 John 5:4*, "For whosoever is born of God overcometh the world: and this is the victory that overcometh the world, even our faith. Who is he that overcometh the world, but he that believeth that Jesus is the Son of God"

If yes, on the next few pages there is a list of scriptures to help you to **establish** a relationship with the God and become a citizen of the Kingdom through receiving His only begotten Son Jesus who is the Christ.

As I have shared with you about the subject "The Working of Faith", the only way that you can experience and walk in blessing of God is by receiving the Lord Jesus Christ as your own personal Lord and Savior.

Jesus said "except you are born again yea shall not see the Kingdom of God" according to **John 3:3**.

If you desire to experience "The Victory that overcometh the world" that were covered in this booklet and in the Holy Bible, you must be born-again in order to qualify to enjoy the victory that overcometh the world. According to **1 John 5:4, 5;**

Are you born again?

Listed are some scripture references that you can check out in the Bible to verify what we are saying. There is a short prayer that you can pray to receive the Lord Jesus Christ as your own personal Lord and Savior, and when you do that, you will be born into the Kingdom of God.

Are you born again? Have you ever received Jesus as your Lord and Savior? If the answer to this question is no, read these scriptures and pray this prayer, agreeing with it and believing it from your heart

John 3:16 "For God so loved the world, that he gave his only begotten Son, that whosoever believeth in him should not perish, but have everlasting life"

Romans 10:9-10, 13 "That if thou shalt confess with thy mouth the Lord Jesus, and shalt believe in thine heart that God hath raised him from the dead, thou shalt be saved.

For with the heart man believeth unto righteousness; and with the mouth **Confession** is made unto salvation. For whosoever shall call upon the name of the Lord shall be saved.

John 14:6 " Jesus said unto him, I am the way, the truth and the life: no man cometh unto the Father, but by me."

PRAY THIS PRAYER

Dear God in Heaven, I come to you believing that Jesus Christ died on the cross for man's sins. I open my heart and invite Jesus to come in to be my personal Lord and Savior. Jesus, forgive me for all my sins and cleanse me from all unrighteousness. Teach me God's Word, and fill me with the power of the Holy Spirit. Give me knowledge and wisdom, and show me how to live a victorious life. I thank You, Jesus, because I am born again and saved through your shed blood on the cross at Calvary. I am on my way to heaven in the name of Jesus.

Signed _____

Date _____

About the Author

Pastor James L. Monteria is born again. He was called into the ministry, and ordained by Faith Christian Fellowship, International of Tulsa, Oklahoma. To effectively execute the call on his life, he attended Rhema Bible Training Center of Broken Arrow a suburb of Tulsa, Oklahoma where he earned a Diploma in Pastoral Training.

Pastor Monteria received his Bachelors of Science Degree in Business Administration from Saint Paul's College in Lawrenceville, VA. He received a Master's Degree in Instructional Education from Central Michigan University, Mount Pleasant, Michigan.

Pastor Monteria has ministered the Word of God through seminars, church services, Bible studies, Prison Ministries, distributions of his books, CD's and DVD's. Pastor Monteria believes that the Bible is the Word of God, and he is an anointed Pastor and Teacher of the Word of God.

His ministries are combination of anointed Preaching and Teaching the Word of God; and flowing in the gifts of the Holy Spirit as the lead.

Pastor J. L. Monteria is available

~Speaking Engagements~ ~Book Signings~
~Workshops\Conferences~

You may contact J L Monteria via

Postal Mail:
Post Office Box 932
Chesterfield, Va 23832

Website:
www.CLM Ministries.org

Email:
Comeandlearnofme@gmail.com

www.ingramcontent.com/pod-product-compliance
Lightning Source LLC
Chambersburg PA
CBHW080548170426
43195CB00016B/2711